CHSPE Math Section Workbook for California High School Proficiency Exam Preparation:
350 Math Review Questions with Step-by-Step Solutions

CHSPE Math Section Workbook for California High School Proficiency Exam Preparation: 350 Math Review Questions with Step-by-Step Solutions

ISBN: 9798376783030

NOTE: The CHSPE is a partnership of the California Department of Education, Sacramento County Office of Education, and Educational Data Systems. The California Department of Education, Sacramento County Office of Education, and Educational Data Systems are not affiliated with nor endorse this publication.

TABLE OF CONTENTS

Mathematics Formula Sheet

Weight
1 ounce ≈ 28.350 grams
1 pound = 16 ounces
1 pound ≈ 453.592 grams
1 milligram = 0.001 grams
1 kilogram = 1,000 grams
1 kilogram ≈ 2.2 pounds
1 ton = 2,000 pounds

Volume
1 cup = 8 fluid ounces
1 quart = 4 cups
1 gallon = 4 quarts
1 gallon = 231 cubic inches
1 liter ≈ 0.264 gallons
1 cubic foot = 1,728 cubic inches
1 cubic yard = 27 cubic feet
1 board foot = 1 inch by 12 inches by 12 inches

Distance
1 foot = 12 inches
1 yard = 3 feet
1 mile = 5,280 feet
1 mile ≈ 1.61 kilometers
1 inch = 2.54 centimeters
1 foot = 0.3048 meters
1 meter = 1,000 millimeters
1 meter = 100 centimeters
1 kilometer = 1,000 meters
1 kilometer ≈ 0.62 miles

Midpoint Formula
$(x_1 + x_2) \div 2 , (y_1 + y_2) \div 2$

Point-Slope Formula
$y - y_1 = m(x - x_1)$

Slope formula
rise/run = $y_2 - y_1 / x_2 - x_1$

Slope-intercept formula
$y = mx + b$
m is the slope of the line and b is the y-intercept

x and y intercepts
$y = 0$ for the x intercept
$x = 0$ for the y intercept

Pythagorean Theorem
$$C = \sqrt{A^2 + B^2}$$

Distance formula
$$d = \sqrt{(x_2 - x_1)^2 + (y_2 - y_1)^2}$$

Factorials
Multiply the number before the exclamation point by every non-zero integer less than that number.
Example: $5! = 5 \times 4 \times 3 \times 2 \times 1$

Combinations
$N! \div [S!(N - S)!]$ where N equals the number of items in the set and S equals the selection size.

Permutations
$N! \div (N - S)!$ where N equals the number of items in the set and S equals the selection size.

Mean (arithmetic average)
To find the mean, add up all of the items in the set and then divide by the number of items in the set.
Consider the data set 5, 2, 4, 1, 3
There are 5 numbers in the set.
Add them together and divide by 5:
$(5 + 2 + 4 + 1 + 3) \div 5 = 3$

Median
Consider the data set 5, 2, 4, 1, 3
Put the numbers in ascending order:
5, 4, **3**, 2, 1
Find the one that is in the middle: 3

Mode
The mode is the number that occurs the most frequently in the set.
Consider the data set 5, 5, 2, 4, 1, 3
The mode is 5 because it occurs twice but the other numbers only occur once.

Range
High value minus low value
Consider the data set 5, 2, 4, 1, 3
Range: $5 - 1 = 4$

Probability

Probability = E ÷ SS; E is the event or the number of items available for the desired outcome; SS is the sample space or the total number of items available in the set.

Example: In a standard deck of playing cards, what is the chance of drawing a diamond?

Answer: There are 52 cards in a standard deck of cards. This is the sample space. There are 13 diamonds in a standard deck of cards. This is the event. Probability = 13 ÷ 52 = ¼

Area

1 square foot = 144 square inches
1 square yard = 9 square feet
1 acre = 43,560 square feet

Circle

(Use 3.14 for the value of π)
number of degrees in circle = 360°
circumference $\approx$ 3.14 × *diameter*
area $\approx$ 3.14 × (*radius*)^2

Triangle

sum of angles = 180°
area = ½ (*base* × *height*)

Rectangle

perimeter = 2(*length* + *width*)
area = *length* × *width*

Rectangular Solid (Box)

volume = *length* × *width* × *height*

Cube

volume = (*length of side*)^3

Cylinder

volume $\approx$ 3.14 × (*radius*)^2 × *height*

Cone

volume $\approx$ (3.14 × *radius*^{2} × *height*) ÷ 3

Sphere (Ball)

volume $\approx$ 4/3 × 3.14 × *radius*^{3}

Temperature

°C = 0.56(°F − 32) or 5/9(°F − 32)
°F = 1.8(°C) + 32 or (9/5 × °C) + 32

CHSPE Math Practice Test 1 – Number Sense and Operations

You should try to complete the questions in this section without a calculator.

1) A company sells electronics online. The annual sales for the first three years of business were: $25,135, $32,787, and $47,004. What were the total sales for the past three years?
A) $101,326
B) $104,916
C) $104,926
D) $104,944

2) A customer gives the cashier $50 to pay for the items he purchased, which total $41.28. How much change should be given to the customer?
A) $7.82
B) $8.18
C) $8.27
D) $8.72

3) A car salesperson earns a $175 referral fee on every customer who accepts a customer service upgrade. The salesperson referred 8 customers for the service upgrade this month. How much did the salesperson earn in referral fees for the month?
A) $1050
B) $1200
C) $1225
D) $1400

4) An employee's weekly pay is $535.50 and she works 30 hours per week. How much is she paid per hour?
A) $17.83
B) $17.84
C) $17.85
D) $18.34

5) Business losses are represented as negative numbers, while business profits are represented as positive numbers. A business makes the following profits and losses during a four week period: –$286, $953, $1502, and –$107. What was the total business profit or loss during these four weeks?
A) $2,026
B) $2,062
C) $2,080
D) –$2,026

6) Location below sea level is represented as a negative number. The location below sea level of Lake Alto is –35 meters. The location below sea level of Lake Bajo is 62 meters deeper than Lake Alto. What figure represents the location below sea level for Lake Bajo?
A) –97
B) 97
C) –62
D) –27

7) A company has completed 3/5 of a project. What figure below expresses the project completion amount as a decimal number?
A) 0.06
B) 0.60
C) 1.67
D) 3.00

8) A teacher reports attendance as a decimal figure, calculated as the number of students attending divided into the total number of students in the class. This week, the attendance was 0.55. What percentage best represents the attendance for this week?
A) 0.55%
B) 5.50%
C) 55.0%
D) 55.5%

9) An employee has used up 5/14 of his vacation days. Approximately what percentage of vacation days has the employee already used?
A) 0.357%
B) 2.800%
C) 3.571%
D) 35.7%

10) A driver has used 0.75 of the gas he last put in his car. What fraction best represents the amount of gas used?
A) 1/4
B) 2/5
C) 3/5
D) 3/4

11) It is reported that 33% of all new stores close within five years of opening. What fraction best represents this percentage?
A) 1/3
B) 1/4
C) 1/5
D) 2/3

12) A carpet store is offering 45% off in a sale this month. What decimal number below best represents the percentage off?
A) 0.0045
B) 0.0450
C) 0.4500
D) 4.5000

13) A bakery has to pay 36 cents for each pound of flour it buys. It decides to buy $14^{1}/_{4}$ pounds of flour today. How much will it have to pay?
A) $3.60
B) $5.13
C) $5.31
D) $142.50

14) A bookkeeper has just been with a client for 0.35 hours. Approximately how many minutes did the bookkeeper spend with this client?
A) 3.5 minutes
B) 5.8 minutes
C) 21 minutes
D) 35 minutes

15) A flower store charges $24 for a small arrangement of flowers. A customer will get a $5 discount if he or she provides his or her own vase for the small arrangement. This month, there were 12 customers who ordered small arrangements and provided their own vases. How much money in total did the flower store make on arrangements sold to these 12 customers?
A) $228
B) $282
C) $288
D) $348

16) A bricklayer works for a construction company. He laid bricks for 7 hours per day for 4 days on one job. The customer was billed $45 per hour for his work, and he was paid $25 per hour. After the bricklayer's wages have been paid, how much money did the company make for his work on this job?
A) $175
B) $180
C) $315
D) $560

17) A pharmacist owns a local drug store. Last week, she filled 250 prescriptions in 40 hours. Assuming that each prescription takes the same amount of time, how many minutes should it take her to fill a single prescription?
A) 9.6 minutes
B) 6.25 minutes
C) 3.75 minutes
D) 0.16 minutes

18) A truck driver delivered 120 orders this week. She delivered 105 of the orders on time. What percentage of the driver's orders was delivered on time?
A) 0.875%
B) 8.75%
C) 87.5%
D) 0.125%

19) A scientist measures cell growth or attrition. Each day a measurement is taken. Cell growth is represented as a positive figure, while cell attrition is represented as a negative figure. On Monday cell growth was 27, and for all days Tuesday through Friday, cell attrition was 13 per day. What number represents total cell growth or attrition for these five days?
A) 25
B) −25
C) 40
D) −40

3

20) A vegetable farmer works until noon each day. The chart below shows the amounts of cucumbers per hour that she picked one morning:

7:00 to 8:00   23 cucumbers   10:00 to 11:00   24 cucumbers
8:00 to 9:00   25 cucumbers   11:00 to 12:00   22 cucumbers
9:00 to 10:00   26 cucumbers

On average, how many cucumbers did the farmer pick per hour?
A) 23
B) 24
C) 25
D) 26

21) A local company makes one particular kind of concrete. For this concrete, 2 units of sand have to be added to every 3 units of cement powder used. A batch of this concrete that has 66 units of cement powder is being made. How many units of sand should be added to this batch?
A) 2
B) 3
C) 22
D) 44

22) It is company policy that the ratio of employees to supervisors should be 50:1. So, for every 50 employees in a company, there should be 1 supervisor. If there are 255 employees, how many supervisors are there?
A) 1
B) 2
C) 3
D) 5

23) A report shows that 2 out of every 20 employees in a particular company are interested in applying for a promotion. If the company has 480 employees in total, how many employees are interested in applying for a promotion?
A) 20
B) 24
C) 42
D) 48

24) A mechanic spent from 8:10 to 8:22 changing three wheel covers on a car. At this rate, how many wheel covers could he change per hour?
A) 3
B) 5
C) 15
D) 20

25) A fencing company put up $15^2/_8$ yards of fence for one customer and $13^5/_8$ yards of fence for another customer. How many yards of fence did the company put up for both customers in total?
A) $28^3/_8$
B) $28^5/_8$
C) $28^7/_8$
D) $28^7/_{16}$

26) A food company fills gourmet food boxes with various products. So far today, $2^3/_8$ boxes have been filled for one order and $4^1/_8$ boxes have been filled for another order. How many total boxes have been filled so far today?
A) $6^1/_2$
B) $6^1/_4$
C) $6^3/_4$
D) $6^3/_{16}$

27) A customer has just placed an order to have an awning made for his front window. According to the measurements, $5^3/_{16}$ yards of canvas will be needed to make the awning. However, the customer calls later to say that his initial measurement was incorrect, and only $4^1/_{16}$ yards of canvas is actually needed to make the awning. Which fraction below represents the amount by which the amount of canvas has been reduced?
A) $1^1/_8$
B) $1^1/_{16}$
C) $1^1/_{32}$
D) $1^3/_{16}$

28) Certain additives need to be placed in a bottle to make a particular product. The company measures each additive in decimal units, with 1 unit representing the filled bottle. The bottle contains 0.25 units of additive A, 0.50 units of additive B, and 0.10 units of additive C. Which of the following represents, in terms of units, how full the bottle currently is?
A) 08.5
B) 0.85
C) 0.90
D) 0.95

29) A recent survey shows that 50% of your customers rated your service as excellent and 25% rated your service as very good. What percentage below represents the total amount of customers who rated your service either excellent or very good?
A) 25%
B) 50%
C) 75%
D) 85%

30) A customer has just ordered 5 units of a product. Each unit of the product takes $1^1/_4$ hours to make. How much time is needed to make this order?
A) 5 hours and 25 minutes
B) 5 hours and 55 minutes
C) 6 hours and 4 minutes
D) 6 hours and 15 minutes

31) A dressmaker who works in a tailoring shop is trying to decide what setting to use on the sewing machine. She has tried the 1/8 inch stitch but has realized that it is too small. The stitches on the machine are sized in 1/32 increments. What size stitch should she try next?
A) 3/16
B) 5/32
C) 6/16
D) 6/32

32) Amal runs a souvenir store that sells key rings. She can get 50 key rings from her first supplier for 50 cents each. She can get the same 50 keys rings from her second supplier for $30 in total or from her third supplier for $27.50. How much will she pay if she gets the best deal?
A) $25.00
B) $25.25
C) $25.50
D) $27.50

33) A budget hotel charges $45 per night or $280 per week. If a guest stays at the hotel for 9 nights, what is the least that he will pay for his stay?
A) $280
B) $315
C) $325
D) $370

34) The price of an item is normally $15, but customers with a loyalty card can purchase it at the discounted price of $12. What percentage best represents the discount awarded to these customers?
A) 3%
B) 5%
C) 15%
D) 20%

35) A retail ceramics store sells mugs and bowls. It buys one type of mug for $3 and sells it for $9. It uses the same percentage mark up on one type of bowl that it buys for $4. What figure below represents the sales price of the bowl?
A) $6
B) $8
C) $12
D) $16

36) A company got $20 off of an order. This amounted to a 25% discount off the order. What would the company have paid without the discount?
A) $4
B) $5
C) $25
D) $80

37) A company that fabricates cleaning products begins to make the first batch of products on Monday at 10:30 am. The actual production time is 3 hours and 25 minutes. This is followed by a bottling and labeling process that takes 1 hour and 40 minutes and a packaging process that takes a further 26 hours. If production keeps to this schedule, when will the first batch be ready for shipment?
A) Tuesday at 12:30 pm
B) Tuesday at 3:55 pm
C) Tuesday at 5:35 pm
D) Wednesday at 3:55 pm

38) Maria sells soft drinks in a convenience store that she runs. She can buy 240 soft drinks from one supplier for 25 cents each or from a different supplier for $58 for all 240 drinks. Both suppliers are in the same state, so she has to pay a sales tax of 6.5% on either purchase. If she chooses the best price for the soft drinks, including tax, how much will she pay in total?
A) $58.00
B) $60.00
C) $61.77
D) $63.90

39) A picture framing store can make 20 small frames in 4 days or 21 large frames in 3 days. A customer has just placed an order with for 40 small frames and 64 large ones. Approximately how many days will it take to make them all?
A) 7
B) 11
C) 14
D) 17

40) The report on a production order shows that 12.5% of the work has been completed in the past 4 days. If work continues at the same rate, how many more days will be required in order to finish the order?
A) 3
B) 4
C) 28
D) 32

41) Consider the instructions in the chart below, and then answer the question that follows.

| Step 1: Begin with a number N. |
| Step 2: Multiply the number by 3. |
| Step 3: Subtract 4 from the result. |
| Step 4: Divide the result by 8. |

If the result of the calculation is 4, what is the value of N?
A) 1
B) 2
C) 12
D) 64

42) A baker multiplied a recipe by $1/2$ when he should have divided the recipe by 4. Which one of the operations on the erroneous result will correct the error?
A) Divide by $1/2$
B) Multiply by $1/2$
C) Multiply by 2
D) Divide by 4

43) When 1523.48 is divided by 100, which digit of the resulting number is in the tenths place?
A) 1
B) 2
C) 3
D) 4

44) What is the greatest common divisor of the following integers? 204 and 272
   A) 72
   B) 68
   C) 34
   D) 24

45) In a sequence of integers, the first number is N and each number in the sequence thereafter is half of the previous number. If the sixth integer in the sequence is 4, what is the first integer?
   A) 256
   B) 192
   C) 128
   D) 108

46) A recent report states that 72.8% of the work for the shopping center is now completed, and it has taken 182 days to do so. If work continues at the same rate, what fraction of the project will be completed after 43 more days? Put the correct amounts in the spaces provided.
   A) $^{43}/_{225}$
   B) $^{182}/_{225}$
   C) $^{1}/_{10}$
   D) $^{9}/_{10}$

47) Solve: 3.75 + 0.004 + 0.179 = ?
   A) 3.969
   B) 3.933
   C) 0.558
   D) 5.58

48) Terry had 32 baseball cards, but he sold 25 percent of them. How many baseball cards did he sell?
   A) 8
   B) 16
   C) 18
   D) 24

49) Which set has the numbers ordered from least to greatest?
   A) $-^{1}/_{4}$, $^{1}/_{8}$, $^{1}/_{6}$, 1
   B) $-^{1}/_{4}$, 1 , $^{1}/_{8}$, $^{1}/_{6}$
   C) $-^{1}/_{4}$, $^{1}/_{8}$, 1 , $^{1}/_{6}$
   D) $-^{1}/_{4}$, $^{1}/_{6}$, $^{1}/_{8}$, 1

50) A business has sold $^{5}/_{14}$ of its inventory. Approximately what percentage of it inventory has the business sold?
   A) 0.357%
   B) 2.800%
   C) 3.571%
   D) 35.7%

Answers and Explanations for CHSPE Math Practice Test 1

1) The correct answer is C. The problem is asking for the total for all three years, so we add the three figures together: $25,135 + $32,787 + $47,004 = $104,926

2) The correct answer is D. For questions that ask you to calculate the change given to a customer, you need to take the amount of money the customer gives the cashier and subtract the amount of the purchase: $50.00 – $41.28 = $8.72

3) The correct answer is D. Multiplication problems will often include the words 'each' or 'every.' The problem states that the salesperson earns a $175 referral fee on every customer, so the referral fee was earned 8 times this month. We need to multiply the amount of the referral fee by the number of customers to solve: $175 × 8 = $1400

4) The correct answer is C. Division problems will often include the word 'per.' The problem states that the employee works 30 hours per week. So, we divide the total weekly amount by the number of hours to solve: $535.50 ÷ 30 = $17.85

5) The correct answer is B. When you have to add a negative number to a positive number, you are really subtracting. So, add the business profits and subtract the business losses: 953 + 1502 – 286 – 107 = 2062

6) The correct answer is A. In this problem, we need to subtract the excess of the depth of Lake Bajo from the location below sea level of Lake Alto. The location below sea level of Lake Alto is a negative number, so we subtract as follows: –35 – 62 = –97. Remember to express your result as a negative number.

7) The correct answer is B. In order to express a fraction as a decimal, treat the line in the fraction as the division symbol: 3/5 = 3 ÷ 5 = 0.60. Be careful with the decimal placement in your final result.

8) The correct answer is C. To express a decimal number as a percent, move the decimal point two places to the right and add the percent sign: 0.55 = 55.0%

9) The correct answer is D. In order to express a fraction as a percentage, you need to divide and then express the result as a percentage. Step 1 – Treat the line in the fraction as the division symbol: 5/14 = 5 ÷ 14 = 0.357. Step 2 – To express the result from Step 1 as a percentage, we need to move the decimal point two places to the right and add the percent sign: 0.357 = 35.7%

10) The correct answer is D. For your exam, you should be able to recognize the equivalent fractions for commonly-used decimal numbers. If you are unsure, perform division on the answer choices to check: 3/4 = 3 ÷ 4 = 0.75

11) The correct answer is A. For your exam, you should be able to recognize the equivalent fractions for commonly-used percentages. If you are unsure, perform division on the answer choices to check:
1/3 = 1 ÷ 3 = 0.3333 = 33%

12) The correct answer is C. Any given percentage is out of 100%, so we divide by 100 to express a percentage as a decimal. So, move the decimal point two places to the left and remove the percent sign: 45% = 45 ÷ 100 = 0.45

13) The correct answer is B. Express both amounts as decimal numbers and multiply to solve: $14^1/_4$ pounds × 36 cents per pound = 14.25 × 0.36 = $5.13

14) The correct answer is C. There are 60 minutes in an hour, so multiply the minutes in the hour by the decimal number given in the problem to solve: 60 minutes × 0.35 hour = 60 × 0.35 = 21 minutes

15) The correct answer is A. Step 1 – Subtract the discount from the original price: $24 – $5 = $19. Step 2 – Take the result from Step 1 and multiply by the number of units sold: $19 × 12 = $228

16) The correct answer is D. Step 1 – Determine the total number of hours worked: 7 hours per day for 4 days = 7 × 4 = 28 hours. Step 2 – Calculate the profit the company makes per hour. The customer was billed $45 per hour for the employee's work, and he was paid $25 per hour: $45 – $25 = $20 profit per hour. Step 3 – Multiply the total number of hours by the profit per hour to solve: 28 hours × $20 profit per hour 28 × 20 = $560

17) The correct answer is A. Step 1 – Calculate how many minutes there are in 40 hours: 40 hours × 60 minutes per hour = 2400 minutes. Step 2 – Divide the number of prescriptions into the previous result to get the rate: 2400 ÷ 250 = 9.6 minutes per prescription

18) The correct answer is C. The orders that were delivered on time are part of the total order. So, take the number of orders that were delivered on time and divide by the number of total orders: 105 ÷ 120 = 0.875 = 87.5%

19) The correct answer is B. On Monday cell growth was 27, and for all of the days Tuesday through Friday, cell attrition was 13 per day. Step 1 – Cell attrition is a negative number, so perform multiplication to get the total for the four days (Tuesday through Friday): –13 × 4 = –52. Step 2 – On Monday cell growth was 27, so add this to the result from Step 1 to solve: –52 + 27 = –25

20) The correct answer is B. To find the average, you need to find the total, and then divide the total by the number of hours. Step 1 – Find the total: 23 + 25 + 26 + 24 + 22 = 120. Step 2 – Divide the result from Step 1 by the number of hours: 120 ÷ 5 = 24

21) The correct answer is D. Step 1 – Take the 66 units of cement powder for the current batch and divide by the 3 units stated in the original ratio: 22 ÷ 3 = 22. Step 2 – Multiply the result from Step 1 by the 2 units of sand stated in the original ratio to get your answer: 2 × 22 = 44

22) The correct answer is D. The problem states that we are working with a ratio, so the employees and the supervisors form separate groups. Step 1 – Add the two groups together: 50 + 1 = 51. Step 2 – Take the total amount of employees stated in the problem and divide this by the figure calculated in Step 1 to get the number of supervisors: 255 ÷ 51 = 5

23) The correct answer is D. The problem uses the phrase '2 out of every 20 employees' so we know that there are 2 employees who form a subset within each group of 20. Step 1 – Take the total number of employees and divide this by 20: 480 ÷ 20 = 24. Step 2 – Take the result from Step 1 and multiply by the amount in the subset to solve: 24 × 2 = 48

24) The correct answer is C. Step 1 – Calculate the amount of time spent on the initial job to do 3 wheel covers: 8:10 to 8:22 = 12 minutes. Step 2 – Calculate how many minutes are needed to change 1 wheel cover: 12 minutes ÷ 3 = 4 minutes each. Step 3 – Divide the figure from Step 2 into 60 minutes to solve: 60 ÷ 4 = 15

25) The correct answer is C. Step 1 – Add the whole numbers. The whole numbers are the numbers in front of the fractions: 15 + 13 = 28. Step 2 – Add the fractions. If you have two fractions that have the same denominator, you add the numerators and keep the common denominator: 2/8 + 5/8 = 7/8. Step 3 – Combine the results from Step 1 and Step 2 to get your new mixed number to solve the problem: 28 + 7/8 = 28$^7/_8$

26) The correct answer is A. Step 1 – Add the whole numbers: 2 + 4 = 6. Step 2 – Add the fractions. If you have two fractions that have the same denominator, you add the numerators and keep the common denominator: 1/8 + 3/8 = 4/8. Step 3 – Simplify the fraction from Step 2: 4/8 = (4 ÷ 4)/(8 ÷ 4) = 1/2. Step 4 – Combine the results from Step 1 and Step 3 to get your new mixed number to solve the problem: 6 + 1/2 = 6$^1/_2$

27) The correct answer is A. Step 1 – Subtract the whole numbers: 5 – 4 = 1. Step 2 – Subtract the fractions. If you have two fractions that have the same denominator, you subtract the numerators and keep the common denominator: 3/16 – 1/16 = 2/16. Step 3 – Simplify the fraction from Step 2: 2/16 = (2 ÷ 2)/(16 ÷ 2) = 1/8. Step 4 – Combine the results from Step 1 and Step 3 to get your new mixed number to solve the problem: 1 + 1/8 = 1$^1/_8$

28) The correct answer is B. Add the three figures together to solve: 0.25 + 0.50 + 0.10 = 0.85. Remember to be sure to put the decimal point in the correct place when you work out the solution to problems like this one.

29) The correct answer is C. Add the percentages together to solve: 25% + 50% = 75%

30) The correct answer is D. Step 1 – Multiply the whole numbers: 5 × 1 = 5. Step 2 – Multiply the whole number by the fraction: 5 × 1/4 = 5/4. Step 3 – Convert the fraction from Step 2 to a mixed number: 5/4 = 1$^1/_4$. Step 4 – Combine the results from Step 1 and Step 3 to get your new mixed number: 5 + 1$^1/_4$ = 6$^1/_4$. Step 5 – Convert the result from Step 4 to hours and minutes: 6$^1/_4$ hours = 6 hours and 15 minutes

31) The correct answer is B. Step 1 – Convert the first fraction to the common denominator: 1/8 = (1 × 4)/(8 × 4) = 4/32. Step 2 – Add one more increment to this to get your result: 4/32 + 1/32 = 5/32

32) The correct answer is A. Step 1 – Work out the cost for the first supplier: 50 units × $0.50 = $25. Step 2 – Compare to other deals to solve: The other deals are $27.50 and $30, so $25 is the best deal.

33) The correct answer is D. Step 1 – Determine the duration of the stay in weeks and nights: 9 nights = 1 week + 2 nights. Step 2 – Add the cost for 1 week to the cost for 2 days to solve: $280 + (2 × $45) = $280 + $90 = $370

34) The correct answer is D. Step 1 – Determine the dollar value of the discount: $15 – $12 = $3. Step 2 – Divide the result from Step 1 by the original price to get the percentage: $3 ÷ $15 = 0.20 = 20%

35) The correct answer is C. Step 1 – Determine the dollar value of the markup on the mug: $9 retail price – $3 cost = $6 markup. Step 2 – Calculate the percentage of the markup by dividing the dollar value of the markup by the cost: $6 ÷ $3 = 2.00 = 200%. Step 3 – Use the percentage markup from the previous step to determine the dollar value of the markup on the bowl: $4 × 200% = $4 × 2 = $8. Step 4 – Add the dollar value of the markup for the bowl to the cost of the bowl to get the retail price: $8 + $4 = $12

36) The correct answer is D. To calculate a reverse percentage you need to divide, rather than multiply. So, take the $20 discount and divide by the 25% percentage: $20 ÷ 25% = $20 ÷ 0.25 = $80

37) The correct answer is C. Step 1 – Add the times for the first two processes and express in terms of hours and minutes: Production time of 3 hours and 25 minutes + Bottling and labeling time of 1 hour and 40 minutes = 3 hours + 1 hour + 25 minutes + 40 minutes = 4 hours and 65 minutes = 5 hours and 5 minutes. Step 2 – Add the time for the packaging process of 26 hours to the result from Step 1: 5 hours and 5 minutes + 26 hours = 31 hours and 5 minutes. Step 3 – Determine the time that the batch will be ready for shipment. 31 hours and 5 minutes have passed. In other words, a period of 24 hours and an additional 7 hours and 5 minutes have passed. The process started on Monday at 10:30 am, so by Tuesday at 10:30 am, 24 hours will have passed. An additional 7 hours and 5 minutes takes us to Tuesday at 5:35 pm.

38) The correct answer is C. Step 1 – Determine the cost from the first supplier: 240 × 0.25 = $60. The tax on this will be $60 × 6.5% = $60 × 0.065 = $3.90. Then add the tax to the cost to get the total: $60 + $3.90 = $63.90. Step 2 – Determine the total cost from the second supplier: $58 cost + ($58 × 0.065 tax) = $58 + 3.77 = $61.77. So, you will get the better deal from the second supplier at $61.77.

39) The correct answer is D. Step 1 – Determine how many days are needed to make the small frames. 20 small frames can be made in 4 days: 20 frames ÷ 4 days = 5 small frames per day. The customer wants 40 small frames, so divide by the rate to determine how many days are going to be needed for the small frames: 40 frames ÷ 5 per day = 8 days. Step 2 – Determine how many days are going to be needed to make the large frames. 21 large frames can be made in 3 days: 21 ÷ 3 = 7 large frames per day. 64 large frames need to be made for the order: 64 ÷ 7 = 9.1 days. Step 3 – Add the results from the two previous steps to solve: 8 days + 9.1 days = 17.1 days, which we round down to 17 days.

40) The correct answer is C. Step 1 – Calculate the percentage of work completed per day. 12.5% of the work has been completed in 4 days: 12.5 % ÷ 4 days = 3.125% per day. Step 2 – Determine how many days in total are needed to complete the entire job by dividing 100% by the result from the previous step: 100% ÷ 3.125% = 32 days. Step 3 –

Determine the number of days remaining: 32 days in total – 4 days completed = 28 days remaining

41) The correct answer is C. Work backwards, using inverse operations. So, if you are asked to divide you multiply to get the solution. If you are asked to subtract, you add to get the solution, and so on. Step 4 says "divide by 8," so multiply our final result of 4 by 8 to perform the first inverse operation: 4 × 8 = 32. Step 3 says "subtract 4," so add 4 to our previous result to perform the inverse operation: 32 + 4 = 36. Step 2 says "multiply by 3," so divide by 3 to perform the final inverse operation to solve: 36 ÷ 3 = 12

42) The correct answer is B. The baker should have divided the recipe by 4. Dividing by four is the same as multiplying by $1/4$. The baker erroneously multiplied by $1/2$, so he needs to multiply by $1/2$ again since $1/2 \times 1/2 = 1/4$.

43) The correct answer is B. This question assesses your understanding of place value. Remember that the number after the decimal is in the tenths place, the second number after the decimal is in the hundredths place, and the third number after the decimal is in the thousandths place. Perform the division, and then check the decimal places of the numbers. Divide as follows: 1523.48 ÷ 100 = 15.2348 Reading our result from left to right: 1 is in the tens place, 5 is in the ones place, 2 is in the tenths place, 3 is in the hundredths place, 4 is in the thousandths place, and 8 is in the ten-thousandths place.

44) The correct answer is B. The greatest common divisor is the largest number that will divide into at least two other numbers. Here our greatest common divisor is 68 since 204 ÷ 68 = 3 and 272 ÷ 68 = 4. If you feel stuck, divide by the first obvious number you can think of, and keep dividing until you can't do any further division. For example, first you could divide by 4: 204 ÷ 4 = 51 and 272 ÷ 4 = 68. Then see if you can divide further. Be sure to consider the prime numbers as possible divisors. Both 51 and 68 from above are divisible by 17, so divide as shown: 51 ÷ 17 = 3 and 68 ÷ 17 = 4..Then multiply the individual divisors together to get the greatest common divisor: 4 × 17 = 68

45) The correct answer is C. When you are given the final term in a sequence and asked for a previous term, you need to divide by the size of the increment to solve. Here, our increment is one-half. Remember to divide by the size of the increment to solve. Again, our increment is one-half. When we divide by one-half, we need to multiply by two since $1 \div \frac{1}{2} = 2$. So, multiply like this to solve: Term 6: 4; Term 5: 4 × 2 = 8; Term 4: 8 × 2 = 16; Term 3: 16 × 2 = 32; Term 2: 32 × 2 = 64; Term 1: 64 × 2 = 128

46) The correct answer is D. As mentioned above, divide the percentage by the number of days in order to determine what percentage of the project is being completed each day: 72.8% ÷ 182 days = 0.4 percent completed per day. For the numerator of the fraction, we need to add 43 more days to the current 182 days: 182 + 43 = 225. Then determine how many days are needed to complete the entire project for the denominator of the fraction.

Since a complete project would be 100% complete, we divide the percentage per day into 100% to get the total days needed: 100% ÷ 0.4 = 250 days. Finally, express this as a simplified fraction:

$$\frac{225}{250} \div \frac{25}{25} = \frac{9}{10}$$

47) The correct answer is B. Be sure to line all of the decimals up in a column like this and then add:

3.750
0.004
0.179
—
3.933

48) The correct answer is A. For this problem, you must perform multiplication: 32 × 0.25 = 8.00

49) The correct answer is A. In order to answer questions on ordering numbers from least to greatest or greatest to least, remember these principles: (a) Negative numbers are less than positive numbers; and (b) When two fractions have the same numerator, the fraction with the smaller number in the denominator is the larger fraction. According to the principles above, $-\frac{1}{4}$ is less than $\frac{1}{8}$, $\frac{1}{8}$ is less than $\frac{1}{6}$, and $\frac{1}{6}$ is less than 1.

50) The correct answer is D. In order to express a fraction as a percentage, you need to divide and then express the result as a percentage. Step 1 – Treat the line in the fraction as the division symbol: 5/14 = 5 ÷ 14 = 0.357 Step 2 – To express the result from Step 1 as a percentage, we need to move the decimal point two places to the right and add the percent sign: 0.357 = 35.7%

CHSPE Math Practice Test 2 – Statistics, Algebra, and Basic Geometry

1) A student receives the following scores on his exams during the semester: 89, 65, 75, 68, 82, 74, 86. What is the mean of his scores?
   A) 24
   B) 74
   C) 75
   D) 77

2) Members of a book club share with each other summaries of the books they have read every month. During the month, the individual members read the following numbers of books. 1, 1, 3, 2, 4, 3, 1, 2, and 1. What is the mode of the number of books read for the entire club?
   A) 1 book
   B) 2 books
   C) 3 books
   D) 4 books

3) Mark's record of times for the 400 meter freestyle at swim meets this season is: 8.19, 7.59, 8.25, 7.35, and 9.10. What is the median of his times?
   A) 7.59
   B) 8.19
   C) 8.25
   D) 8.096

4) Find the median of the following data set: 10, 12, 8, 2, 5, 21, 8, 6, 2, 3
   A) 7
   B) 6.5
   C) 2
   D) 19

5) A student receives the following scores on her assignments during the term: 98.5, 85.5, 80.0, 97, 93, 92.5, 93, 87, 88, 82. What is the range of her scores?
   A) 17.0
   B) 18.0
   C) 18.5
   D) 89.65

6) What is the mode of the numbers in the following list? 1.6, 2.9, 4.5, 2.5, 5.1, 5.4
   A) 3.5
   B) 3.1
   C) 3.0
   D) no mode

7) Ten children are attending a weekly activity with their parents. Nine of the children have the following ages: 2, 3, 4, 5, 6, 7, 9, 10, and 12 years old. If the average age of the 10 children is 6 years old, how old is the 10th child?
   A) 1 year old
   B) 2 years old

C) 3 years old
D) 4 years old

8) 100 participants took an intelligence test. The mean score for the first 50 participants was 82, and the mean score for the next 50 participants was 89. What is the mean test score for all 100 participants?
A) 85.5
B) 86.5
C) 87
D) 88

9) An employee at the Department of Motor Vehicles wanted to find the mean of the ten driving theory tests he administered this morning. However, the employee divided the total points from the ten tests by 8, which gave him an erroneous result of 78. What is the correct mean of the ten tests?
A) 97.5
B) 70
C) 62.4
D) 52

10) X is 5 times Y, and Y is 5 more than 4 times Z. Which of the following describes the relationship between X and Z?
A) X is 25 more than 20 times Z.
B) X is 5 more than 5 times Z.
C) X is 5 more than 20 times Z.
D) X is 25 more than 5 times Z.

11) Given sets A, B, and C below, which of the following represents A U (B ∩ C)?

A = {1, 2, 3, 4, 5}
B = {1, 3, 5, 7, 9}
C = {7, 9, 11, 49, 81, 121}

A) {7, 9}
B) {1, 2, 3, 4, 5}
C) {1, 2, 3, 4, 5, 7, 9}
D) {1, 2, 3, 4, 5, 7, 9, 11, 49, 81, 121}

12) A local bingo hall has 10 extra-large bingo cards, 15 large bingo cards, 20 medium bingo cards, and 30 small bingo cards before any players arrive. Players are given a bingo card from the box at random upon arrival. The first player received an extra-large card and the second player received a small card. What is the probability that the next player will receive a medium card?
A) $^{18}/_{73}$
B) $^{20}/_{73}$
C) $^{18}/_{75}$
D) $^{20}/_{75}$

13) The school soccer team has played 10 matches so far this season. Their scores were: 6, 7, 3, 0, 1, 5, 4, 8, 2, 4. What is the mean of their scores?
A) 3.5
B) 4
C) 8
D) 40

14) A report shows that 3 out of every 8 workers in a certain factory are dissatisfied with their pay. If the factory has 520 workers in total, how many of them are dissatisfied with their pay?
A) 325
B) 65
C) 165
D) 195

15) $60 - {}^{3x}/_5 \geq 36$, then x ≤ ?
A) 40
B) 60
C) 80
D) 120

16) You need to test a 0.82 gram sample of an active liquid ingredient. How many milligrams of liquid should you test?
A) 0.00082
B) 0.0082
C) 82.0
D) 820

17) A car dealership has cars, pickups, vans, and SUVs. At the start of the financial quarter, they have a total of 1,500 vehicles. The table below shows percentages by category for the 1,500 vehicles at the start of the quarter. At the end of the year, the dealership still has 1,500 vehicles, but cars constitute 40%, pickups 21%, and SUVs 16%.

Cars	42%
Pickups	17%
Vans	26%
SUVs	15%

What can be said about the number of vans at the end of the quarter when compared to the number of vans at the beginning of the quarter?
A) There were 23 more vans at the end of the quarter.
B) There were 23 fewer vans at the end of the quarter.
C) There were 45 more vans at the end of the quarter.
D) There were 45 fewer vans at the end of the quarter.

18) Samira is going to buy a mobile home. The total purchase price of the mobile home, including interest and finance charges, is represented by variable H. She will pay Q dollars upfront, and then she will make equal payments (P) each month for a certain number of months (N). Her monthly payment (P) can be represented by which of the following equations?

A) $(H-Q)/N$

B) $H/N - Q$

C) $N/(H-Q)$

D) $Q-H/N$

19) What is the value of $-7 \times 2 - 12 \div 4$?
   A) -17
   B) -11
   C) 11
   D) 17

20) Determine the slope of the line with the following sets of coordinates: $(-1, 2)$ and $(4, 3)$
   A) $1/5$
   B) -1
   C) -5
   D) 5

21) Shanice can ride 3 miles on her bike in 25 minutes. If she maintains this pace, how long will it take her to ride her bike 9 miles?
   A) 50 minutes
   B) 1 hour and 15 minutes
   C) 1 hour and 25 minutes
   D) 1 hour and 30 minutes

22) The amount of snowfall in Cedar Valley during one week, measured to the nearest quarter inch per day, is provided in the following list: 0.75, 0.25, 1.00, 0.00, 0.50, 0.25, 1.50
What is the median amount of snowfall for this week?
   A) 0.50
   B) 1.25
   C) 1.46
   D) 1.50

23) A basketball hoop is 18 wide. What is the distance around the outside of the hoop?
   A) 81π
   B) 36π
   C) 18π
   D) 9π

24) The graph below shows the number of accidents in four different counties during a two-year period. Which county had the greatest increase in accidents from last year to this year?

Accident Rates in 4 Counties

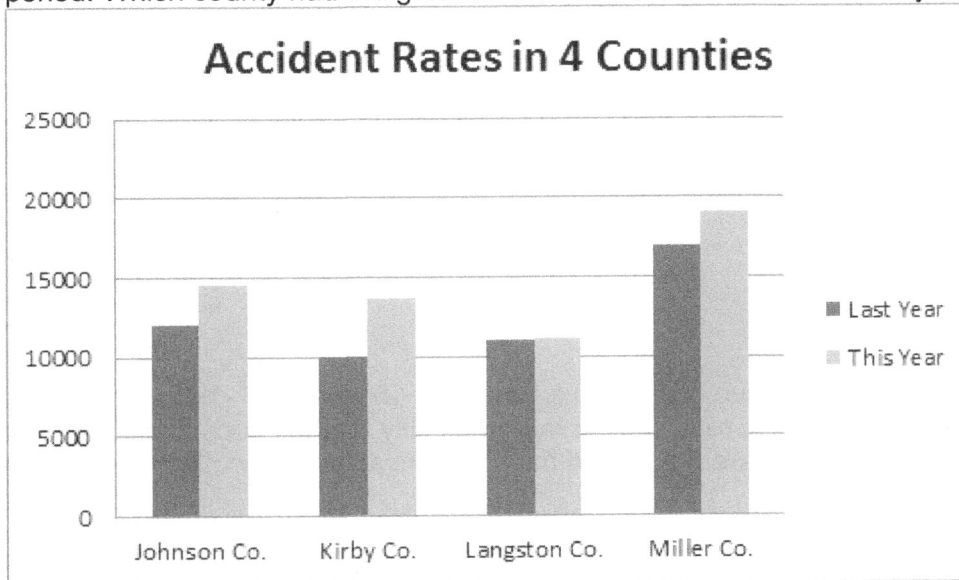

A) Johnson
B) Kirby
C) Langston
D) Miller

25) Express the following equation of a line in slope-intercept form: 6x + 8y = 24
A) $y = -\,^x/_4 + 8$
B) $y = \,^x/_4 + 8$
C) $y = -\,^{3x}/_4 + 3$
D) $y = \,^{3x}/_4 + 3$

26) The distance between two markings on a racecourse is 723 feet. What is the approximate distance between the markings in meters?
A) 220
B) 1,166
C) 2,372
D) 7,230

27) The two lines represented by the equations below intersect in the xy-plane. What is the y-coordinate at the point of intersection?
2x – 3y = 37
x = 5
A) –3.5
B) 3.5
C) –9
D) 9

28) A field has an area of exactly 49 square feet. Which one of the following could be the length (L) and width (W) of the field?
A) L = 14.5; W = 10
B) L = 7; W = 7
C) L = 10; W = 5
D) L = 18; W = 15

29) Which of the following is equivalent to $(x^2 \times x^4)^3$?
A) x^9
B) x^{11}
C) x^{18}
D) x^{24}

30) A lottery spinner contains 7 blue balls, 8 pink balls, and 15 white balls before any balls are drawn. If the first ball drawn is pink, what is the probability that the second ball drawn will also be pink? Note that balls are not placed back into the spinner once they have been drawn.
A) $^7/_{29}$
B) $^7/_{30}$
C) $^8/_{29}$
D) $^8/_{30}$

31) Cylinder C is a right-angled cylinder. The radius (R) of the base of cylinder is 6 inches. The height of the cylinder is 10 inches. What is the volume of the cylinder in cubic inches?
A) 36π
B) 140π
C) 360π
D) 720π

32) The table below shows the percentages of total residents of Central City suffering from different illnesses last year. There were 231,000 total residents in Central City last year.

Illness Rates in Central City Last Year

Illness	Percentage
Pneumonia	11%
Bronchitis	17%
Sinus Infection	32%
Influenza	48%

Approximately how many residents of Central City did not get influenza last year?
A) 24,480
B) 110,880
C) 120,120
D) 110,480

33) Given sets D, E, and F below, which of the following represents (D ∩ E) U F?
D = {0, 2, 4, 6, 8, 10}
E = {1, 2, 4, 8, 18, 36}
F = {2, 12, 22, 32}

A) {2}
B) {2, 4, 8}
C) {2, 12, 22, 32}
D) {2, 4, 8, 12, 22, 32}

34) Statistics reveal that the average 4-person household consumes 4.5 alcoholic drinks per week and 10 soft drinks per week. The 4-person households in one particular town consume 841 soft and alcoholic drinks per week. How many 4-person households are there in this town?
A) 3784
B) 186
C) 58
D) 84.1

35) In December, the ratio of bags of apples to bags of oranges in a grocery store is 2 to 12. If there are 14 bags of apples in the store, how many bags of oranges are there?
A) 28
B) 48
C) 84
D) 96

36) A box contains 7 orange tickets, 8 green tickets, 6 red tickets, and 11 purple tickets. If a ticket is drawn from the box at random, what is the probability that it will be green?
A) $^1/_4$
B) $^1/_6$
C) $^1/_8$
D) $^1/_{32}$

37) Which of the following is equivalent to y^{-8}?
A) $-1 \times y^8$
B) $1 \div y^8$
C) $-1 + y^8$
D) $-1 - y^8$

38) In the standard (x, y) plane, what is the distance between (2, –2) and (6, 4)?
A) $\sqrt{52}$
B) 52
C) 10
D) $^3/_2$

39) A prison administrator needs to calculate the area of the floor of a prison cell. He has determined that the cell is 14 feet long and 9 feet wide. However, he needs to convert the area to square yards for record-keeping purposes. What is the area of the prison cell in terms of square yards?
A) 4 square yards
B) 7 square yards

C) 14 square yards
D) 126 square yards

40) Factor the following: $ab^4c^3 + a^2b^2c^4 - a^2b^2c^2 - ab^2c^3$
   A) $ab^2c(b^2c + ac^2 - a - c)$
   B) $ab^2c^2(b^2c + ac^2 - a + c)$
   C) $ab^2c^2(b^2c + ac^2 - a - c)$
   D) $abc^2(b^2c + ac^2 - a - c)$

41) For the functions $f_1(x)$ below, x is a negative integer less than −10 and y is a positive integer greater than 100. If $f_1(x) = x^2$, which of the functions below has the largest value for $f_2(f_1(x))$?
   A) $f_2(x) = x + y$
   B) $f_2(x) = (xy)^2$
   C) $f_2(x) = xy$
   D) $f_2(x) = x - y$

42) What is the value of $f_1(4)$ where $f_1(x) = 3^x$?
   A) 64
   B) 12
   C) 81
   D) 4^4

43) Which of the following best describes the range of $y = x^2 - 52$?
   A) All real numbers.
   B) $y \geq 0$
   C) $y \leq -52$
   D) $y \geq -52$

44) What are two possible values of x for the following equation?
   $x^2 + 5x + 6 = 0$
   A) −2 and −3
   B) −5 and −6
   C) 5 and 6
   D) 2 and 3

45) If $f(x) = x \div (3 + x)$ and $g(x) = 1 \div (x - 2)$, what is the domain of the function $f + g$?
   A) $\{-3, 0\}$
   B) All real numbers.
   C) All real numbers except 0.
   D) All real numbers except −3 and 2.

46) If $f(x) = x^2 + 4x + 2$, what is $f(x + 3)$
   A) $x^2 + 10x + 14$
   B) $(x + 3)^2 + 4(x + 3) + 2$
   C) $(x + 3)^2 + 4x + 5$
   D) $(x + 3)^2 + 4(x + 3)^2 + 2$

47) For the two functions $f_1(x)$ and $f_2(x)$, tables of values are given below. What is the value of $f_2(f_1(2))$?

x	$f_1(x)$
1	3
2	5
3	7
4	9
5	11

x	$f_2(x)$
2	4
3	9
4	16
5	25
6	36

A) 1
B) 25
C) 5
D) 2

48) Solve for x: $4x = \log_{11}121$
A) $^1/_2$
B) 30.25
C) 2
D) 1

49) $a \neq b, \dfrac{6a/b}{3a/a+b}$

Where $a \neq b$, which of the following is an equivalent expression?

A) $\dfrac{18a^2}{ab+b^2}$

B) $\dfrac{3a}{a}$

C) $\dfrac{2a-2ab}{b}$

D) $\dfrac{2a+2b}{b}$

50) For which of the following is x = 3 one of the solutions?
A) $x^2 - 10x + 21 = 0$
B) $(x + 3)^2$
C) $x^2 + 2x - 3 = 0$
D) $x^2 - 3x - 4 = 0$

Answers and Explanations for CHSPE Math Practice Test 2

1) The correct answer is D. To find the mean, add up all of the items in the set and then divide by the number of items in the set. Here we have 7 numbers in the set, so we get our answer as follows: $(89 + 65 + 75 + 68 + 82 + 74 + 86) \div 7 = 539 \div 7 = 77$

2) The correct answer is A. The mode is the number that occurs the most frequently in the set. Our data set is: 1, 1, 3, 2, 4, 3, 1, 2, 1. The number 1 occurs 4 times in the set, which is more frequently than any other number of books read, so the mode is 1.

3) The correct answer is B. The problem provides the number set: 8.19, 7.59, 8.25, 7.35, 9.10 First of all, put the numbers in ascending order: 7.35, 7.59, 8.19, 8.25, 9.10. Then find the one that is in the middle: 7.35, 7.59, **8.19**, 8.25, 9.10

4) The correct answer is A. Put the numbers is ascending order: 2, 2, 3, 5, **6**, **8**, 8, 10, 12, 21. Here, we have got an even number of items, so we need to take an average of the two items in the middle: $(8 + 6) \div 2 = 7$

5) The correct answer is C. To calculate the range, the low number in the set is deducted from the high number in the set. The problem set is: 98.5, 85.5, 80.0, 97, 93, 92.5, 93, 87, 88, 82. The high number is 98.5 and the low number is 80, so the range is 18.5 ($98.5 - 80 = 18.5$).

6) The correct answer is D. The mode is the number that occurs most frequently. However, if no number occurs more than once, the set has no mode.

7) The correct answer is B. The age of the 10th child is our unknown variable, so set up an equation to calculate the average and put this in as x to solve:
$(2 + 3 + 4 + 5 + 6 + 7 + 9 + 10 + 12 + x) \div 10 = 6$
$[(2 + 3 + 4 + 5 + 6 + 7 + 9 + 10 + 12 + x) \div 10] \times 10 = 6 \times 10$
$2 + 3 + 4 + 5 + 6 + 7 + 9 + 10 + 12 + x = 60$
$58 + x = 60$
$x = 2$

8) The correct answer is A. Find the total points for the first group: $50 \times 82 = 4100$. Then find the total points for the second group. $50 \times 89 = 4450$. Add these two amounts together for the total points: $4100 + 4450 = 8550$. Then divide the total points by the total number of members in the group: $8550 \div 100 = 85.5$

9) The correct answer is C. First, multiply the erroneous average by the erroneous number of tests to get the total points: $78 \times 8 = 624$. Then divide this total by the correct amount: $624 \div 10 = 62.4$

10) The correct answer is A. The problem tells us that X is 5 times Y, and Y is 5 more than 4 times Z. So, we need to create equations based on this information.
X is 5 more than 4 times Z: $X = 4Z + 5$
X is 5 times Y: $X = 5Y$
Since $Y = 4Z + 5$, we can substitute $4Z + 5$ for Y in the second equation as follows:
$X = 5Y$
$X = 5(4Z + 5)$

X = 20Z + 25
So X is 25 more than 20 times Z.

11) The correct answer is C. The question is asking for the union of A with the intersection of B and C. Since (B ∩ C) is in parentheses, we need to find that intersection first. Remember that ∩ is the intersection, so you need to find the items that are common to both sets. On the other hand, U is the union, so you have to combine the sets for the union.
Look at sets B and C and highlight the numbers that they have in common:
B = {1, 3, 5, **7**, **9**}
C = {**7**, **9**, 11, 49, 81, 121}
So (B ∩ C) = {7, 9}
Set A before the union with this intersection was A = {1, 2, 3, 4, 5}.
So add the numbers from (B ∩ C) to set A to get your answer:
{1, 2, 3, 4, 5, 7, 9}

12) The correct answer is B.
Find the total of all of the bingo cards at the start: 10 + 15 + 20 + 30 = 75
The first player received an extra-large card and the second player received a small card, so subtract 2 cards from the above figure to find out how many cards are left: 75 − 2 = 73
This number goes in the denominator of the fraction that we are going to make.
We want to know the chance of getting a medium card. No medium cards have been handed out at this point, so we still have 20 medium cards left.
Put the number of medium cards in the numerator to solve: $^{20}/_{73}$

13) The correct answer is B. The mean is the same thing as the arithmetic average.
The scores were: 6, 7, 3, 0, 1, 5, 4, 8, 2, 4
So, first we add them together:
6 + 7 + 3 + 0 + 1 + 5 + 4 + 8 + 2 + 4 = 40
Then divide by the number of matches to get the mean:
40 ÷ 10 = 4

14) The correct answer is D. The problem uses the phrase '3 out of every 8 workers' so we know that there are 3 workers who form a subset within each group of 8.
Step 1 – Take the total number of workers and divide this by 8:
520 ÷ 8 = 65
Step 2 – Take the result from Step 1 and multiply by the amount in the subset to solve:
65 × 3 = 195

15) The correct answer is A.
First, isolate the whole numbers.
$60 - {}^{3x}/_5 \geq 36$
$(60 - 60) - {}^{3x}/_5 \geq 36 - 60$
$-{}^{3x}/_5 \geq -24$
Then get rid of the denominator on the fraction.
$-{}^{3x}/_5 \geq -24$
$(5 \times -{}^{3x}/_5) \geq -24 \times 5$
$-3x \geq -24 \times 5$
$-3x \geq -120$

Then isolate the remaining whole numbers.
$-3x \geq -120$
$-3x \div 3 \geq -120 \div 3$
$-x \geq -120 \div 3$
$-x \geq -40$
Then deal with the negative number.
$-x \geq -40$
$-x + 40 \geq -40 + 40$
$-x + 40 \geq 0$
Finally, isolate the unknown variable as a positive number.
$-x + 40 \geq 0$
$-x + x + 40 \geq 0 + x$
$40 \geq x$
$x \leq 40$

16) The correct answer is D. Convert 0.82 grams to milligrams.
1 milligram = 0.001 grams, so 0.82 grams ÷ 0.001 = 820 milligrams

17) The correct answer is D. We have to calculate the percentage of vans at the end of the quarter by subtracting the percentages for the other categories: 100% – 40% – 21% – 16% = 23%. The percentage of vans was 26% at the start of the quarter and 23% at the end of the quarter, so there was a 3% decrease. We can then multiply to solve: 1,500 × 0.03 = 45 fewer vans at the end of the quarter

18) The correct answer is A. The total amount that Samira has to pay is represented by H. She is paying Q dollars immediately upfront, so we can determine the remaining amount that she owes by deducting her down payment from the total. So, the remaining amount owing is represented by the equation: H – Q. We have to divide the remaining amount owing by the number of months (N) to get the monthly payment (P): $P = (H - Q) \div N = \frac{H - Q}{N}$

19) The correct answer is A. Do the multiplication and division from left to right. So, take the number to the left of the multiplication or division symbol and multiply or divide that number by the number on the right of the symbol. We need to multiply –7 by 2 and then divide –12 by 4. You can see the order of operations more clearly if you put in parentheses to group the numbers together: $-7 \times 2 - 12 \div 4 = (-7 \times 2) - (12 \div 4) = -14 - 3 = -17$

20) The correct answer is A. Our coordinates are: (–1, 2) and (4, 3)
The formula for slope is: $rise/run = \frac{y_2 - y_1}{x_2 - x_1}$
Substitute the values for the coordinates: $\frac{3 - 2}{4 - -1} = \frac{1}{5}$

21) The correct answer is B. Shanice rides 3 miles in 25 minutes, so in order to determine how long she needs to ride 9 miles, we multiply 25 by 3. In other words, since she rides 3 miles in 25 minutes, she will need three times as long to ride 9 miles (since 3 times 3 equals 9). 25 minutes × 3 = 75 minutes; 75 minutes = 1 hour and 15 minutes

22) The correct answer is A. The median is the number that is in the middle of a data set when the values are placed in ascending order. Order the numbers to solve:
0.00, 0.25, 0.25, **0.50**, 0.75, 1.00, 1.50. When the numbers are in order, we can see that the answer is 0.50.

23) The correct answer is C. The question is simply asking you to calculate the circumference. The formula for circumference is: Circumference = π × diameter
The diameter is the same as the width, so substitute 18 to solve: π × 18 = 18π

24) The correct answer is B. We can see from the chart that Langston County had very little change. Miller County increased by approximately 2,000, while Johnson increased by approximately 3,000. Kirby County increased by approximately 4,000, so B is the correct answer.

25) The correct answer is C. The slope intercept form is: y = mx + b
m is the slope of the line and b is the y-intercept.
The y-intercept of the line is the value of the point where the line crosses the y axis.
Our original equation was: 6x + 8y = 24
Isolate y to express the equation in slope-intercept form:
6x + 8y = 24
8y = −6x + 24
8y ÷ 8 = (−6x + 24) ÷8
y = $^{-6x}/_8$ + 3
Divide the numerator and the denominator of the fraction by 2 in order to simplify:
y = $^{-6x}/_8$ + 3
y = $^{-3x}/_4$ + 3

26) The correct answer is A. From the formula, we can see that 1 foot = 0.3048 meters.
To solve, multiply the amount of 723 feet, stated in the question, by 0.3048:
723 × 0.3048 = 220.3704
We round this down to 220.

27) The correct answer is C.
We have two equations:
2x − 3y = 37
x = 5

Substitute 5 for x in the first equation to solve for y:
2x − 3y = 37
(2 × 5) − 3y = 37
10 − 3y = 37
10 − 10 − 3y = 37 − 10
−3y = 27
−3y ÷ −3 = 27 ÷ −3
y = −9

28) The correct answer is B. The area of a rectangle or square is: L × W
Performing the operations, we can see the following: 7 × 7 = 49

29) The correct answer is C. The exponents on the x variables should be added together, but the exponent outside the parentheses needs to be multiplied by the new exponent.
Add the exponents on the variables together:
$(x^2 × x^4)^3$ =
$(x^{2 + 4})^3$ =
$(x^6)^3$

27

The exponent outside the parentheses is then multiplied by the new exponent from the previous step:
$(x^6)^3 =$
$x^{(6 \times 30)} =$
x^{18}

30) The correct answer is A. Find the total of all of the balls before any have been removed: $7 + 8 + 15 = 30$. Find the number of balls available after the first draw: $30 - 1 = 29$ Probability is a fraction, and the number above will be our denominator. We want to know the chance of getting a pink ball on the second draw. There were 8 pink balls at the start and one has been removed, so 7 pink balls are left. So, put the number of pink balls in the numerator to solve: $^7/_{29}$

31) The correct answer is C. Volume of cylinder $= \pi R^2 h = \pi \times radius^2 \times height$
In our problem, R = 6 and h = 10: $\pi R^2 h = \pi 6^2 \times 10 = 36\pi \times 10 = 360\pi$

32) The correct answer is C. Find the percentage for the patients that did not get the illness: $100\% - 48\% = 52\%$. Then multiply that percentage by the total number of residents to solve: $231,000 \times 52\% = 120,120$

33) The correct answer is D. The question is asking for the union of F with the intersection of D and E. Find the intersection first. Highlight the numbers that sets D and E have in common:
D = {0, **2**, **4**, 6, **8**, 10}
E = {1, **2**, **4**, **8**, 18, 36}
So D ∩ E = {2, 4, 8}
Set F before the union with this intersection was F = {2, 12, 22, 32}.
The 2 is already in set F, so add the 4 and the 8 to solve:
{2, 4, 8, 12, 22, 32}

34) The correct answer is C. Step 1 – Add the number of soft and alcoholic drinks per week: $10 + 4.5 = 14.5$. Step 2 – Divide the result from Step 1 into the total drinks to solve: $841 \div 14.5 = 58$

35) The correct answer is C. The ratio of bags of apples to bags of oranges is 2 to 12, so for every two bags of apples, there are twelve bags of oranges. First, take the total amount of bags of apples and divide by the 2 from the original ratio: $14 \div 2 = 7$
Then multiply this by 12 to determine how many bags of oranges are in the store:
$7 \times 12 = 84$

36) The correct answer is A. Find the total of all of the tickets, which we call the items in the "sample space": $7 + 8 + 6 + 11 = 32$. We express probability as a fraction, and the number above will be our denominator. We want to know the chance of getting a green ticket, so put the number of green tickets in the numerator and simplify: $^8/_{32} = {}^{[8 \div 8]}/_{[32 \div 8]} = ¼$

37) The correct answer is B. Remember that a negative exponent is always equal to 1 divided by the variable. Therefore, $y^{-8} = 1 \div y^8$

38) The correct answer is A. To solve the problem, you need to use the distance formula:
$$d = \sqrt{(x_2 - x_1)^2 + (y_2 - y_1)^2}$$

Put in the values provided, which were between (2, –2) and (6, 4). Then multiply and simplify to solve:

$\sqrt{(x_2 - x_1)^2 + (y_2 - y_1)^2} =$

$\sqrt{(6 - 2)^2 + (4 - -2)^2} =$

$\sqrt{(4)^2 + (6)^2} =$

$\sqrt{16 + 36} =$

$\sqrt{52}$

39) The correct answer is C. Step 1 – Find the area in terms of square feet first. You need to multiply the feet together first to get square feet and then do the conversion to square yards.
Rectangular area = length × width
14 × 9 = 126 square feet
Step 2 – Convert the area in square feet to square yards (1 square yard = 9 square feet): The formula converts square yards to square feet, but we are converting square feet to square yards, so we need to divide by the conversion factor.
So, divide by 9 to convert to yards:
126 ÷ 9 = 14 square yards

40) The correct answer is C. Factor the polynomial variable by variable. Our expression is:
$ab^4c^3 + a^2b^2c^4 - a^2b^2c^2 - ab^2c^3$
We can see that each term has variable a or greater. So factor out variable a:
$ab^4c^3 + a^2b^2c^4 - a^2b^2c^2 - ab^2c^3 =$
$a(b^4c^3 + ab^2c^4 - ab^2c^2 - b^2c^3)$
Each of the terms inside the parentheses has b^2 or greater, so factor out b^2:
$a(b^4c^3 + ab^2c^4 - ab^2c^2 - b^2c^3) =$
$ab^2(b^2c^3 + ac^4 - ac^2 - c^3)$
For the terms that remain inside the parentheses, each term has c^2 or greater. Factor out c^2:
$ab^2(b^2c^3 + ac^4 - ac^2 - c^3) =$
$ab^2c^2(b^2c + ac^2 - a - c)$

41) The correct answer is B. $f_1(x)$ is the function in the inner parentheses, so the value calculated for $f_1(x)$ will be used for the variable x in the function $f_2(x)$. $(xy)^2$ will always be greater than xy, x – y or x + y since we get a positive number when multiplying two negative numbers for x^2. Accordingly, the result will be greatest when xy is squared. If you are unsure, insert values for x and y to test the result.

42) The correct answer is C. Put the value provided for x into the function to solve.
$f_1(x) = 3^x$
$f_1(4) = 3^x$
$3^4 = 81$

43) The correct answer is D. The range of a function is all possible y values or "outputs" for the function. $x^2 - 52$ will yield a result of –52 when x = 0. $x^2 - 52$ will result in a number greater than –52 for all other positive or negative values of x. Therefore, the range will always be equal to or greater than –52.

29

44) The correct answer is A. Step 1: Factor the equation. First of all, look at the third term of the equation, which is 6. We need to find the factors of 6:

$1 \times 6 = 6$ and $2 \times 3 = 6$.

The second term of the equation contains a 5, so we need two factors that add up to five. Choose 2 and 3 since $2 + 3 = 5$.

Then factor the equation like this:

$x^2 + 5x + 6 = 0$

$(x + 2)(x + 3) = 0$

Step 2: Now substitute 0 for x in the first pair of parentheses.

$(0 + 2)(x + 3) = 0$

$2(x + 3) = 0$

$2x + 6 = 0$

$2x + 6 - 6 = 0 - 6$

$2x = -6$

$2x \div 2 = -6 \div 2$

$x = -3$

Step 3: Then substitute 0 for x in the second pair of parentheses.

$(x + 2)(x + 3) = 0$

$(x + 2)(0 + 3) = 0$

$(x + 2)3 = 0$

$3x + 6 = 0$

$3x + 6 - 6 = 0 - 6$

$3x = -6$

$3x \div 3 = -6 \div 3$

$x = -2$

45) The correct answer is D.

Remember that the domain of a function is all possible x values for the function.

You need to avoid any mathematical operations that do not have real number solutions, such as dividing by a zero or finding the square root of a negative number.

$f(x) = x \div (3 + x)$, so to avoid dividing by a zero, $x \neq -3$

$g(x) = 1 \div (x - 2)$, so $x \neq 2$

To find the domain of both functions, put these two results together to state the exclusions to the domain.

Therefore, the domain of $f + g$ is all real numbers except -3 and 2.

46) The correct answer is B. Substitute $(x + 3)$ for x in the original function to solve:

So, $x^2 + 4x + 2$ becomes: $(x + 3)^2 + 4(x + 3) + 2$

47) The correct answer is B. Looking at the first table for the value of $f_1(2)$, we can see on the second line of the table that $f_1(2) = 5$. Then use 5 as the value of x in the second function. Looking at the second table for the value of $f_2(5)$, we can see on the fourth line of the table that $f_1(5) = 25$.

48) The correct answer is A. $4x = \log_{11}121$ is the same as $11^{4x} = 121$ and $11^2 = 121$, so the result of the exponent needs to be equal to 2. The exponent in the question is 4x, so $x = 0.5$ or $^1/_2$.

49) The correct answer is D. When you have fractions in the numerator and denominator of another fraction, you can divide the two fractions as follows:

$$\frac{6a/b}{3a/a+b} = \frac{6a}{b} \div \frac{3a}{a+b}$$

Then invert and multiply just like you would for any other fraction

$$\frac{6a}{b} \div \frac{3a}{a+b} = \frac{6a}{b} \times \frac{a+b}{3a} =$$

$$\frac{6a(a+b)}{b(3a)} = \frac{6a^2 + 6ab}{3ab}$$

Then simplify, if possible.

$$\frac{6a^2 + 6ab}{3ab} = \frac{3a(2+2b)}{3a(b)} =$$

$$\frac{\cancel{3a}(2+2b)}{\cancel{3a}(b)} = \frac{2a+2b}{b}$$

50) The correct answer is A. Our equation was: $x^2 - 10x + 21 = 0$. Step 1 – Look at the third term of the equation, which is 21. Find two integers that equal 21 when multiplied. $1 \times 21 = 21$; $3 \times 7 = 21$; $-3 \times -7 = 21$; $-1 \times -21 = 21$. Step 2 – Look at the second term of the equation, which is $-10x$. Find two integers from Step 1 that equal -10 when they are added. $-3 + -7 = -10$. Step 3 – Use the integers -3 and -7 to factor our quadratic. $(x - 3)(x - 7) = 0$. Step 4 – Substitute 0 for x in each of the parentheticals to find possible solutions.

$(0 - 3)(x - 7) = 0$
$-3(x - 7) = 0$
$-3(7 - 7) = 0$
$x = 7$

$(x - 3)(0 - 7) = 0$
$(x - 3) \times -7 = 0$
$(3 - 3) \times -7 = 0$
$x = 3$

1) A land surveyor must measure the distance between landmarks. She has measured a distance between two landmarks and discovered that it is 538 feet. What is the approximate distance between the landmarks in terms of meters?
   A) 45
   B) 164
   C) 1367
   D) 1765

2) A physical therapist measures how far her clients are able to walk during each session. One client walked 123 feet and 6 inches during his first session and 138 feet and 8 inches during his second session. What is the combined total of the distance walked for the two sessions?
   A) 261 feet 24 inches
   B) 261 feet 6 inches
   C) 262 feet 8 inches
   D) 262 feet 2 inches

3) A nutritionist advises clients and sells supplements to them. A box containing the supplements weighs 8 pounds and 5 ounces when full. The box itself weighs 7 ounces when it is empty. Each supplement weighs 0.75 ounces. About how many supplements should be in the box?
   A) 168
   B) 177
   C) 178
   D) 186

4) A garden store fertilizes and treats customers' lawns. One customer wants to fertilize and treat his lawn, which is $50^1/_4$ feet by $60^1/_4$ feet in size. The cost of the fertilizer and treatment is $5.25 per square yard. To the nearest dollar, how much will it cost the customer to fertilize and treat his lawn?
   A) $177
   B) $1,766
   C) $5,298
   D) $15,895

5) It is company policy to have at least 60 yards of dark black yarn in stock at the start of every month. Inventory has been taken this morning and there are 2 balls of dark black yarn that are 75 inches each and 4 balls of dark black yarn that are $25^1/_4$ inches each in stock. This yarn must be purchased in 5-yard-long balls. How many balls of yarn should be purchased in order to replenish the stock?
   A) 10
   B) 11
   C) 33
   D) 36

6) A company that manufactures liquid cosmetics needs to test a 0.75 gram sample of an active ingredient of a liquid cosmetic. The correct concentration ratio is 50 milligrams of active ingredient to 1.5 milliliters of liquid. How many milliliters of liquid should be added to the sample?
A) 0.000015
B) 0.000225
C) 15.0
D) 22.5

7) Find the midpoint of the line segment that connects the points (5, 2) and (7, 4).
A) (6, 3)
B) (3, 6)
C) (3.5, 5.5)
D) (12, 6)

8) If store A is represented by the coordinates (−4, 2) and store B is represented by the coordinates (8,−6), and store A and store B are connected by a line segment, what is the midpoint of this line?
A) (2, 2)
B) (2, −2)
C) (−2, 2)
D) (−2, −2)

9) What is the distance between (2, 3) and (6, 7)?
A) 4
B) 16
C) $\sqrt{16}$
D) $\sqrt{32}$

10) The measurements of a mountain can be placed on a two-dimensional linear graph on which $x = 5$ and $y = 315$. If the line crosses the y axis at 15, what is the slope of this mountain?
A) 60
B) 63
C) 300
D) 315

11) State the x and y intercepts that fall on the straight line represented by the equation:
$y = x + 14$
A) (−14, 0) and (0, 14)
B) (0, 14) and (0, −14)
C) (14, 0) and (0, −14)
D) (0, −14) and (14, 0)

12) Find the x and y intercepts of the following equation: $x^2 + 2y^2 = 144$
A) (12, 0) and (0, $\sqrt{72}$)
B) (0, 12) and ($\sqrt{72}$, 0)
C) (0, $\sqrt{72}$) and (0, 12)
D) (12, 0) and ($\sqrt{72}$, 0)

13) A carpenter creates triangular-shaped corner shelves from oak and other wood for sale to furniture and home stores. He needs to report the area of each shelf to the buyer as part of the sales agreement. He needs to calculate the area of a triangular-shaped shelf that has a base of 12 inches and a height of 14 inches. What is the area of this shelf in square inches?
A) 56
B) 84
C) 168
D) 1728

14) Triangle ABC is a right-angled triangle. Side A and side B form the right angle, and side C is the hypotenuse. If A = 3 and B = 2, what is the length of side C?
A) 5
B) $\sqrt{5}$
C) $\sqrt{13}$
D) 13

15) A carpenter is making a special triangular-shaped corner shelf for a custom order. The customer lives in a 300-year-old house, so the walls are not completely straight and the corners are not completely square. He needs to make a triangular shelf that will have one 44° angle and one 47° angle. What is the measurement in degrees of the third angle of this shelf?
A) 45°
B) 45.5°
C) 89°
D) 90°

16) A real-estate developer has recently purchased a circular-shaped tower. The first floor of the building has been divided into 5 pie-shaped segments that join at the center of the circle. The first segment measures 82° along the outside edge. The second segment has a measurement of 79°, the third has a measurement of 46° and the fourth has a measurement of 85°. What is the measurement in degrees of outside edge the fifth segment?
A) 48
B) 49
C) 58
D) 68

17) A building project has a circular tower. The floor of the tower, which has a 12-foot radius, needs to be filled in with concrete. In order to do this, the area of the floor of the tower needs to be calculated. What is the approximate area of the floor of the tower in square feet?
A) 452.16
B) 376.80
C) 226.08
D) 37.68

18) A technician measures the wear on tractor tires. In order to determine the rate of wear, the circumference of each tire must be determined first. The tire currently being measured has a diameter of 46.5 inches. What is the circumference?
   A) 23.500 inches
   B) 73.005 inches
   C) 146.01 inches
   D) 292.02 inches

19) Becky is making a patchwork quilt that is going to be 6 feet long and 5 feet wide. What will the surface area of the quilt be in square feet?
   A) 11
   B) 22
   C) 25
   D) 30

20) A fence needs to be put around a field that is 12 yards long and 9 yards wide. What figure below best represents the perimeter of this field in yards?
   A) 21
   B) 42
   C) 54
   D) 72

21) A circular fish pond is being designed for your local park. The pond has an area of about 78.5 square feet. What is the approximate diameter of the pond?
   A) 5 feet
   B) 10 feet
   C) 15.7 feet
   D) 25 feet

22) A rectangular vegetable garden has an area of 360 square feet. If the length of the garden is 30 feet, what is the width of the garden?
   A) 12 feet
   B) 24 feet
   C) 115 feet
   D) 150 feet

23) A tank that holds dye is 5 feet wide, 8 feet long, and 3 feet high. How many cubic feet of dye can the tank hold when it is completely full?
   A) 15
   B) 24
   C) 40
   D) 120

24) A cube footrest has a side length of 18 inches. How many cubic inches of filling should be placed inside the footrest?
   A) 5,832
   B) 729
   C) 324
   D) 72

25) A company processes dairy products. Milk is stored in a spherical storage tank that is 72 inches across on the inside at its widest point. The tank is now 80% full of milk. What is the volume of the milk in the tank?
A) 156,267
B) 156,627
C) 159,333
D) 195,333

26) A cylindrical tank has a 5 meter radius and is 21 meters in height. What is the volume of the tank?
A) 329.70
B) 1648.5
C) 549.50
D) 659.40

27) A confection company manufactures three different sizes of ice cream cones. The large cones are 6 inches high and have a 1.5 inch radius, the medium cones are 5 inches high and have a 1 inch radius, and the small cones are 4 inches high and have a 0.5 inch radius. What is the difference between the volume in cubic inches of the large cone and the medium cone?
A) 4.19
B) 5.23
C) 8.90
D) 14.13

28) A building contractor is laying wooden parquet pieces on a floor. The wooden part of the floor will cover an area that measures 8 feet long by 4 feet wide. Each wooden parquet piece measures 12 inches by 6 inches. What is the minimum number of wooden parquet pieces that will be needed in order to cover the wooden part of the floor?
A) 16
B) 32
C) 48
D) 64

29) A painter is painting a wall that is 16 feet long and 11 feet high. She needs to calculate the surface area of the wall in order to know how much paint to buy. What is the surface area of the wall in square feet?
A) 54
B) 121
C) 176
D) 256

30) A gardener is mowing a yard that is 35 feet long and 20 feet wide. What is the surface area of the yard in square feet?
A) 55
B) 110
C) 700
D) 1400

31) A beaker is cylindrical and measures 18 inches high and 12 inches in diameter. However, the volume has to be converted from cubic inches to gallons for a report. What is the approximate volume of the beaker in terms of gallons?
A) 2.9 gallons
B) 8.8 gallons
C) 10.4 gallons
D) 8,138.88 gallons

32) A beaker is cylindrical and measures 18 inches high and 12 inches in diameter. However, the volume has to be converted from cubic inches to gallons for a report. What is the approximate volume of the beaker in terms of gallons?
A) 2.9 gallons
B) 8.8 gallons
C) 10.4 gallons
D) 8,138.88 gallons

33) A company ships products overseas in large rectangular shipping containers. One type of container is 25 feet long, 12 feet wide, and 18 feet high. The container is currently 75% full of a particular product. What is the volume in cubic yards of the product in the container?
A) 150 cubic yards
B) 200 cubic yards
C) 405 cubic yards
D) 4,050 cubic yards

34) A company manufactures glue and other adhesives that contain a chemical called PVA. At least 50 quarts of PVA need to be in stock at the start of every month. Inventory has been taken this morning and there are 2 containers of PVA that hold 16 cups and 7 ounces each. There are also 3 containers of PVA that hold 20 cups and 4 ounces each. This PVA must be purchased in 5-quart containers. How many containers are needed in order to replenish the stock?
A) 0
B) 5
C) 6
D) 7

35) A company that manufactures hand soap and laundry detergent has to order liquid parabens that are used in its products. The parabens are stored in two identically sized vats. The vats measure 10 feet by 10 feet by 12 feet. The first vat is $^3/_4$ full and the second vat is $^4/_5$ full. The parabens cost 12 cents a cubic inch. To the nearest dollar, what is the cost value of the parabens in the two vats?
A) $223
B) $3,857
C) $4,977
D) $385,690

36) A company that manufactures batteries stores acid in a conical-shaped container that is 6 feet in diameter and 8 feet in height. The manager has calculated that the inside of the container at its maximum could contain approximately 226 cubic feet of acid. What error, if any, has been made in this calculation?
A) There is no error in the calculation.
B) The manager forgot to divide by 3.
C) The manager forgot to multiply by 3.14.
D) The manager squared the container's diameter instead of its radius.

37) An electrician installs wiring and lighting in new homes. The client would like to install lights on the walls in the living room. The living room is 25 feet long and 10 feet wide. The client would like a light to be installed on each wall in 5-foot increments. However, no lights are to be installed in the corners of the room. How many lights will be needed in order to carry out this job?
A) 8
B) 10
C) 12
D) 14

38) A company that manufactures ice cubes and frozen refreshments makes two sizes of ice cubes. The large ice cubes have a side length of 1.8 millimeters, and the small ice cubes have a side length of 1.4 millimeters. What is the amount in cubic millimeters of the difference in volume between the large ice cube and the small one?
A) 0.064
B) 1.960
C) 2.744
D) 3.088

39) A building engineer has been asked to calculate the areas of two triangular shapes. The large triangle has a base of 12 inches and a height of 18 inches. The small triangle has a base of 8 inches and a height of 14 inches. What is the difference in the areas of the two shapes?
A) 8
B) 16
C) 25
D) 52

40) If a circle with center $(-5, 5)$ is tangent to the x axis in the standard (x, y) coordinate plane, what is the diameter of the circle?
A) −5
B) −10
C) 5
D) 10

41) Results from a questionnaire administered to customers of a particular grocery store show that 4 out of 7 customers prefer toffee-flavored ice cream to coffee-flavored ice cream. Based on these results, if 1,540 customers purchased one of these two flavors of ice cream, how many of them would have purchased coffee-flavored ice cream?
    A) 220
    B) 420
    C) 560
    D) 660

42) A measurement of 116 feet is how many inches longer than a measurement of 36 yards?
    A) 8
    B) 80
    C) 96
    D) 960

43) Susan is trying to limit her caffeine intake. She has a coffee in the morning every third day and a glass of iced tea every fourth day in the afternoon. For how many of the next 90 days will Susan consume coffee and iced tea on the same day?
    A) 7
    B) 10
    C) 12
    D) 22

44) In a particular section of a library, the ratio of non-fiction books to fiction books is 7 to 9. The total number of fiction and non-fiction books in this section of the library is 128. If 10 fiction books and 14 non-fiction books are retired and removed from this section of the library, what fraction of the remaining books in this section are fiction?
    A) 56/72
    B) 42/62
    C) 62/42
    D) 31/52

45) The following three locations are on a map of an amusement park: Ferris wheel, roller coaster, and entrance. On the map, which is drawn to scale, the distance between the Ferris wheel and the entrance is 8 inches, and the distance between the entrance and the roller coaster is 6.5 inches. The actual distance between the Ferris wheel and the entrance is 350 yards. What is the actual distance between the entrance and the roller coaster to the nearest yard?
    A) 294
    B) 284
    C) 350
    D) 360

46) In the standard (x, y) plane, what is the distance between $(4\sqrt{7}, -2)$ and $(7\sqrt{7}, 4)$?
    A) $3\sqrt{11}$
    B) 27
    C) 36
    D) 99

47) The information provided in the box below describes three locations on a map. Use the information provided to answer the question that follows.

- The police station is 10 miles away from the fire station
- The fire station is 6 miles away from the hospital.

Based on the information in the box, what conclusions can be made?
A) The police station is no more than 6 miles away from the hospital.
B) The police station is no more than 10 miles away from the hospital.
C) The police station is exactly 6 miles away from the hospital.
D) The police station is no more than 16 miles away from the hospital.

48) In the figure below, lines 1 and 2 are parallel. What is the measurement of angle y in degrees?

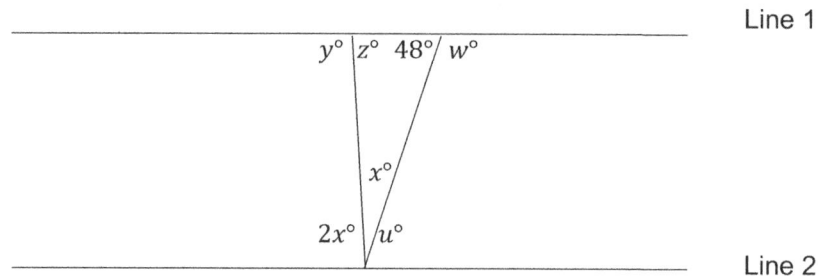

A) 48
B) 44
C) 88
D) 92

49) Consider rectangular figure WXYZ below:

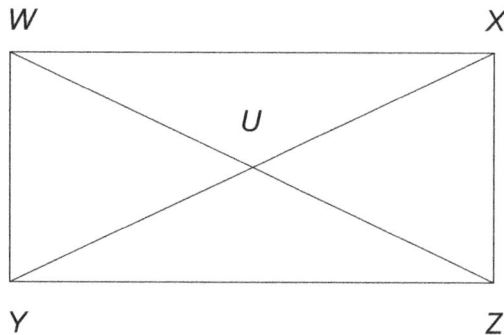

Which of the following must be true?
A) $\angle YWX \cong \angle YWU$
B) $\angle YUW \cong \angle WUX$
C) $\overline{WY} \cong \overline{UY}$
D) $\overline{WY} \cong \overline{XZ}$

50) In the Venn diagram below, circle *A* represents the integers from 3 to 13 inclusive, and circle B represents the integers 5 to 15 inclusive. How many integers are represented in region C of the diagram?

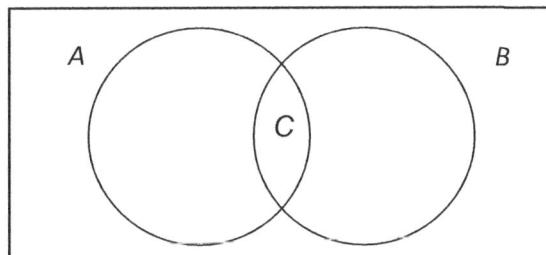

A) 2
B) 8
C) 9
D) 10

Answers and Explanations for CHSPE Math Practice Test 3

1) The correct answer is B. From the formula, we can see that 1 foot = 0.3048 meters. To solve, multiply the amount of 538 feet, stated in the question, by 0.3048: 538 × 0.3048 = 163.98, which we round up to 164.

2) The correct answer is D. Step 1 – First of all, add the feet together: 123 + 138 = 261 feet. Step 2 – Add the inches together: 6 + 8 = 14 inches. Step 3 – Convert the inches to feet and inches if the result from Step 2 is 12 inches or more: 14 inches = 1 foot 2 inches. Step 4 – Combine the results from Step 1 and Step 3 to solve: 261 feet + 1 foot 2 inches = 262 feet 2 inches

3) The correct answer is A. Step 1 – Convert the weight of the full box from pounds and ounces to just ounces. We are using the formula 1 pound = 16 ounces, so 8 pounds and 5 ounces = (8 × 16) + 5 = 128 + 5 = 133 ounces. Step 2 – The problem states that the box weighs 7 ounces when it is empty. So, subtract the weight of the empty box from the weight of the full box to get the weight of the product inside the box: 133 ounces – 7 ounces = 126 ounces. Step 3 – The problem tells us that each supplement weighs 0.75 ounces. Take the total weight from the previous step and divide by the weight per unit to determine how many units the box contains: 126 ounces ÷ 0.75 ounces = 168 units

4) The correct answer is B. Step 1 – Convert the mixed numbers to decimals and then multiply: $50\frac{1}{4}$ feet × $60\frac{1}{4}$ feet = 50.25 × 60.25 = 3027.5625 square feet. Step 2 – The price is given in square yards, so convert the square feet from the previous step to square yards. The formula states that 1 square yard = 9 square feet, so 1/9 square yard = 1 square foot: 3027.5625 square feet ÷ 9 = 336.3958 square yards. Step 3 – Calculate the cost: 336.3958 × $5.25 = $1765.92, which we round to $1,766.

5) The correct answer is B. Step 1 – Calculate the amount of remaining stock in inches: (2 × 75 inches) + (4 × 25.25 inches) = 150 + 101 = 251 inches. Step 2 – Convert the existing stock from inches to yards: 1 foot = 12 inches and 1 yard = 3 feet, so there are 36 inches in 1 yard. So, divide the number of inches by 36 to convert to yards: 251 ÷ 36 = 6.97 yards. Step 3 – Calculate the amount required to restock. 60 yards are required in total, and there are 6.97 yards on hand, so subtract to find out how many more yards are needed to get the stock back up to 60 yards: 60 – 6.97 = 53.03 yards needed. Step 4 – The yarn comes in 5-yard balls, so calculate how many balls to buy to cover the 53.03 yards that are required: 53.03 ÷ 5 = 10.6 balls. It is not possible to buy a fractional part of a ball, so we round up to 11 balls.

6) The correct answer is D. Step 1 – Convert 0.75 grams to milligrams. 1 gram = 1,000 milligrams, so 0.75 grams × 1,000 = 750 milligrams. Step 2 – The normal ratio is in the amount of 50 milligrams, so divide the result from the previous step by 50: 750 ÷ 50 = 15. So, 15 times more active ingredient is being used than normal. Step 3 – Determine the amount of liquid. Since 15 times more of the active ingredient is being used, we also need to use 15 times more of the liquid: 1.5 milliliters × 15 = 22.5 milliliters

7) The correct answer is A. Our points are (5, 2) and (7, 4), so substitute the values into the midpoint formula.
$(x_1 + x_2) \div 2$, $(y_1 + y_2) \div 2$
$(5 + 7) \div 2$ = midpoint x, $(2 + 4) \div 2$ = midpoint y

12 ÷ 2 = midpoint x, 6 ÷ 2 = midpoint y
6 = midpoint x, 3 = midpoint y

8) The correct answer is B. First, find the midpoint of the x coordinates for (**−4**, 2) and (**8**,−6).
midpoint $x = (x_1 + x_2) ÷ 2$
midpoint $x = (−4 + 8) ÷ 2$
midpoint $x = 4 ÷ 2$
midpoint $x = 2$
Then find the midpoint of the y coordinates for (−4, **2**) and (8,**−6**).
midpoint $y = (y_1 + y_2) ÷ 2$
midpoint $y = (2 + −6) ÷ 2$
midpoint $y = −4 ÷ 2$
midpoint $y = −2$
So, the midpoint is (2, −2)

9) The correct answer is D. Substitute the values (2, 3) and (6, 7) into the formula.
$$d = \sqrt{(x_2 − x_1)^2 + (y_2 − y_1)^2}$$
$$d = \sqrt{(6 − 2)^2 + (7 − 3)^2}$$
$$d = \sqrt{4^2 + 4^2}$$
$$d = \sqrt{16 + 16}$$
$$d = \sqrt{32}$$

10) The correct answer is A. Substitute the values into the slope-intercept formula.
$y = mx + b$
$315 = m5 + 15$
$315 − 15 = m5 + 15 − 15$
$300 = m5$
$300 ÷ 5 = m5 ÷ 5$
$60 = m$

11) The correct answer is A. Remember that the y intercept is where the line crosses the y axis, so $x = 0$ for the y intercept. Begin by substituting 0 for x.
$y = x + 14$
$y = 0 + 14$
$y = 14$
Therefore, the coordinates (0, 14) represent the y intercept.

On the other hand, the x intercept exists where the line crosses the x axis, so $y = 0$ for the x intercept.
Now substitute 0 for y.
$y = x + 14$
$0 = x + 14$
$0 − 14 = x + 14 − 14$
$−14 = x$
So, the coordinates (−14, 0) represent the x intercept.

12) The correct answer is A. The x intercept is the point at which a line crosses the x axis of a graph. In order for the line to cross the x axis, y must be equal to zero at that particular

43

point of the graph. On the other hand, the *y* intercept is the point at which the line crosses the *y* axis. So, in order for the line to cross the *y* axis, *x* must be equal to zero at that particular point of the graph. First, substitute 0 for *y* in order to find the *x* intercept.

$x^2 + 2y^2 = 144$

$x^2 + (2 \times 0) = 144$

$x^2 + 0 = 144$

$x^2 = 144$

$x = 12$

Then substitute 0 for *x* in order to find the *y* intercept.

$x^2 + 2y^2 = 144$

$(0 \times 0) + 2y^2 = 144$

$0 + 2y^2 = 144$

$2y^2 \div 2 = 144 \div 2$

$y^2 = 72$

$y = \sqrt{72}$

So, the *y* intercept is $(0, \sqrt{72})$ and the *x* intercept is (12, 0).

13) The correct answer is B. From the formula, we can see that the area of a triangle is ½ (base × height). So, substitute the values to solve: ½ (base × height) = ½ (12 × 14) = ½ × 168 = 84 square inches

14) The correct answer is C. Use the Pythagorean Theorem to solve. $C = \sqrt{A^2 + B}$
$C = \sqrt{A^2 + B^2} = \sqrt{3^2 + 2^2} = \sqrt{9 + 4} = \sqrt{13}$

15) The correct answer is C. The sum of the angles in a triangle is 180 degrees. So, subtract the measurements of the other two angles to solve: 180° − 47° − 44° = 89°

16) The correct answer is D. From the formula, we can see that a circle has 360 degrees. So, subtract to solve: 360 − 82 − 79 − 46 − 85 = 68

17) The correct answer is A. From the formula, we can see that the area of a circle ≈ 3.14 × (*radius*)². So, put in 12 feet for the radius to solve: 3.14 × (12 × 12) = 3.14 × 144 = 452.16

18) The correct answer is C. From the formula, we know that the circumference of a circle ≈ 3.14 × diameter. The problem states that the diameter of the tractor tire is 46.5 inches, so use that in the formula to solve: 3.14 × 46.5 = 146.01 inches

19) The correct answer is D. The area of a rectangle = length × width. Your quilt is 6 feet long and 5 feet wide, so multiply to solve: 6 × 5 = 30

20) The correct answer is B. The perimeter of a rectangle = 2(length + width). Your field is 12 yards long and 9 yards wide, so use the formula to solve: 2(12 + 9) = 2 × 21 = 42

21) The correct answer is B. Step 1 – The area of a circle ≈ 3.14 × radius². Here, we are given the area, so we have to divide by 3.14, instead of multiplying by 3.14, as stated in the formula: 78.5 ÷ 3.14 = 25. Step 2 – The result from the previous step is the radius squared. A squared number is the result of a number that has been multiplied by itself. 5 × 5 = 25, so the length of the radius of the pond is 5 feet. Step 3 – Remember that diameter is double the radius, so if the radius is 5, the diameter is 10 feet.

22) The correct answer is A. For questions on rearranging formulas like this one and the previous one, it is very likely that you are going to have to divide the largest number in the question by a smaller number in order to solve the problem. From the formula, we know that the area of a rectangle = length × width. Here, we are given the area (the larger number of 360), so we need to divide that by the length (the smaller number of 30 feet) in order to get the width: 360 ÷ 30 = 12 feet

23) The correct answer is D. The volume of a rectangular solid = length × width × height. The tank is 5 feet wide, 8 feet long, and 3 feet high, so multiply to solve: 5 × 8 × 3 = 120

24) The correct answer is A. A cube is a three-dimensional object in which all sides have the same length. The volume of a cube = side length^3. So, put the length of the side in the formula to solve: 18 × 18 × 18 = 5832

25) The correct answer is A. Step 1 – Calculate in cubic inches the volume of the sphere when it is full. The tank is 72 inches across on the inside, so the radius is 36 inches. The volume of a sphere ≈ 4/3 × 3.14 × radius^3: 4/3 × 3.14 × 36^3 = 195,333.12 cubic inches. Step 2 – Calculate in cubic inches how much milk remains in the sphere. The tank is now 80% full of milk: 195,333.12 cubic inches × 0.80 = 156,266.50 cubic inches, which we round to 156,267 cubic inches.

26) The correct answer is B. The volume of a cylinder ≈ 3.14 × height × radius^2. Your tank has a 5-meter radius and is 21 meters in height: 3.14 × 21 × 5^2 = 3.14 × 21 × 25 = 1648.50 cubic meters

27) The correct answer is C. Step 1 – Calculate the volume of the large cone. The large cones are 6 inches high and have a 1.5 inch radius. The volume of a cone ≈ (3.14 × height × radius^2) ÷ 3 = (3.14 × 6 × 1.5 × 1.5) ÷ 3 = 14.13. Step 2 – Calculate the volume of the medium cone. The medium cones are 5 inches high and have a 1 inch radius: (3.14 × height × radius^2) ÷ 3 = (3.14 × 5 × 1 × 1) ÷ 3 = 5.23. Step 3 – Calculate the difference between the volume of the two cones: 14.13 – 5.23 = 8.90

28) The correct answer is D. Step 1 – Calculate the dimensions of the floor in inches: 8 feet × 12 inches per foot = 96 inches long; 4 feet × 12 inches in a foot = 48 inches wide. Step 2 – Determine how many wooden pieces will fit along the length of the floor. If we lay the 12-inch side of the wooden piece against the length of the room, we can lay 8 of these side by side to cover the 96-inch length: 96 ÷ 12 = 8. Step 3 – Determine how many wooden pieces can fit along the width. 48-inch-wide floor ÷ 6-inch-wide pieces = 48 ÷ 6 = 8 pieces. Step 4 – Multiply the results from steps 2 and 3 to get the total number of pieces needed for the job: 8 × 8 = 64

29) The correct answer is C. area of a rectangle = length × width. The wall is 16 feet by 11 feet, so multiply to solve: 16 × 11 = 176

30) The correct answer is C. To find the area, multiply the length by the width: 35 × 20 = 700

31) The correct answer is B. Step 1 – Find the volume in terms of cubic inches. Remember that radius is half of diameter. Here we have a diameter of 12, so the radius is 6. Cylinder volume ≈ 3.14 × radius^2 × height ≈ 3.14 × 6^2 × 18 ≈ 3.14 × 36 × 18 ≈ 2034.72. Step 2 –

Convert the volume in cubic inches to gallons. 1 gallon = 231 cubic inches, so divide by 231 to convert to gallons: 2034.72 ÷ 231 = 8.8 gallons

32) The correct answer is D. Step 1 – First we need to calculate the volume in terms of cubic feet. The volume of a cube = (length of side)^3. The length of the side is 9 feet, so the volume is 9 × 9 × 9 = 729 cubic feet. Step 2 – We have to convert the result from Step 1 to cubic inches. From the formula, we can see that 1 cubic foot = 1,728 cubic inches, so multiply to solve: 729 × 1,728 = 1,259,712 cubic inches

33) The correct answer is A. Step 1 – Calculate in cubic feet the volume of the container when it is full. The container is 25 feet long, 12 feet wide and 18 feet high. To find the volume of a rectangular solid, we use the formula: length × width × height = 25 × 12 × 18 = 5,400 cubic feet. Step 2 – Calculate in cubic feet how much product is in the container. The container is now 75% full: 5,400 cubic feet × 0.75 = 4,050 cubic feet. Step 3 – Convert the cubic feet to yards. 1 cubic yard = 27 cubic feet. The formula is cubic yards to cubic feet, but you are converting from cubic feet to cubic yards, so you need to divide: 4,050 cubic feet ÷ 27 = 150 cubic yards

34) The correct answer is C. Step 1 – Calculate the amount of remaining stock in quarts and ounces: [2 × (16 cups and 7 ounces)] + [3 × (20 cups and 4 ounces)] = 32 cups and 14 ounces + 60 cups and 12 ounces = 92 cups and 26 ounces. Step 2 – Convert the existing stock from cups to quarts: 1 quart = 4 cups, so divide the number of cups by 4 to convert to quarts: (92 cups ÷ 4) + 26 ounces = 23 quarts and 26 ounces. There are 32 ounces in a quart, so we cannot convert the remaining 26 ounces to quarts. Step 3 – Calculate the amount required to restock. 50 quarts are required in total, and you have approximately 23 quarts on hand, so subtract to find out how many more quarts you need to get the stock back up to 50 quarts: 50 – 23 = 27 quarts needed. Step 4 – The chemical comes in 5-quart containers, so calculate how many containers you need to buy to cover the 27 quarts that are required: 27 ÷ 5 = 5.4 quarts. It is not possible to buy a fractional part of a container, so you have to buy 6 containers.

35) The correct answer is D. Step 1 – Calculate the volume of each vat: length × width × height = 10 × 10 × 12 = 1,200 cubic feet. Step 2 – Determine how full each vat is in terms of cubic feet. Vat 1: 1,200 × $^3/_4$ = 1,200 × 0.75 = 900 cubic feet. Vat 2: 1,200 × $^4/_5$ = 1,200 × 0.80 = 960 cubic feet. Step 3 – Add the volume of the two vats together to determine the total volume: 900 + 960 = 1,860 cubic feet. Step 4 – Convert the cubic feet to cubic inches. 1 cubic foot = 1,728 cubic inches, so we multiply to convert: 1,860 cubic feet × 1,728 = 3,214,080 cubic inches. Step 5 – Multiply by the price to solve: 3,214,080 cubic inches × $0.12 = $385,689.60, which we round to $385,690.

36) The correct answer is B. Step 1 – Calculate the radius of the cone. The diameter is 6 and radius is half of diameter, so the radius is 3. Step 2 – Calculate the correct volume of the cone. The formula for the volume of a cone ≈ (3.14 × radius^2 × height) ÷ 3 = (3.14 × 3^2 × 8) ÷ 3 = 226.08 ÷ 3 = 75.36 cubic feet. Step 3 – Compare the correct figure to the erroneous figure to determine whether the erroneous calculation was too large or too small. You calculated 226 cubic feet, so you erred on the large side.   Step 4 – Identify where the error occurred. We can see from the calculation in step 2 that final part of the calculation of the volume is (3.14 × 3^2 × 8) ÷ 3 = 226.08 ÷ 3, so the manager has forgotten to divide by 3.

37) The correct answer is B. No lights are to be installed in the corners, so each of the two 10-feet walls will have 1 light installed in the middle of each wall: 10 ÷ 5 = 2, but we subtract 1 from this for the corner. So, we have 1 light on each of the 2 shorter walls, which accounts for 2 lights so far. Each of the 25-foot walls have 5 increments of 5 feet, and again no lights are in the corners: (25 ÷ 5) – 1 = 4. So, each of the 2 long walls will have 4 lights on each wall. So, there will be 10 lights in total on the walls in the room (1 + 1 + 4 + 4 = 10). You may wish to draw a diagram on your scratch paper when solving problems like this one.

38) The correct answer is D. Step 1 – Calculate the volume of the large ice cube: (1.8 × 1.8 × 1.8) = 5.832. Step 2 – Calculate the volume of the small ice cube: (1.4 × 1.4 × 1.4) = 2.744. Step 3 – Calculate the difference between the volume of the two ice cubes: 5.832 – 2.744 = 3.088

39) The correct answer is D. Step 1 – Calculate the area of the large triangle: (12 × 18) ÷ 2 = 216 ÷ 2 = 108. Step 2 – Calculate the area of the small triangle: (8 × 14) ÷ 2 = 112 ÷ 2 = 56. Step 3 – Subtract to solve: 108 – 56 = 52

40) The correct answer is D. If the center of a circle (x, y) is tangent to the x axis, then both of the following conditions are true: [1] The point of tangency is equal to (x, 0) and [2] The distance between (x, y) and (x, 0) is equal to the radius. The center of this circle is (−5, 5) and the point of tangency is (−5, 0). We need to subtract these two coordinates in order to find the length of the radius: (−5, 5) − (−5, 0) = (0, 5). In other words, the radius length is 5, so the diameter length is 10.

41) The correct answer is D. Be careful with the phrase "out of" in proportion questions like this one. We are given the phrase "4 out of 7." If 4 out of 7 prefer the toffee flavor, then the remaining 3 prefer the coffee flavor. Accordingly, the ratio of flavor preference of toffee to coffee is 4 to 3. So, after determining the ratio, your next step is to divide the total by 7: 1540 ÷ 7 = 220. Then multiply this by 3 for the coffee-flavor preference: 220 × 3 = 660

42) The correct answer is C. First of all, convert 36 yards to feet: 36 yards × 3 feet in a yard = 108 feet. Then subtract this from 116 feet: 116 – 108 = 8 feet. Then convert the feet to inches for your answer: 8 feet × 12 inches per foot = 96 inches

43) The correct answer is A. For interval questions like this one, multiply the number of days of each interval together to get the day on which the intervals will coincide. Every twelfth day, Susan will have both drinks on the same day. We get this result by multiplying 3 days for the coffee interval by 4 days for the tea interval: 3 × 4 = 12. Then we have to determine how many 12-day intervals there are in 90 days. We do this by dividing 90 by 12: 90 ÷ 12 = 7.5. We don't count the half day, so the answer is 7.

44) The correct answer is D. Add the two parts of the ratio together: 7 + 9 = 16. Then divide this into the total number of books: 128 ÷ 16 = 8. Then multiply each part of the ratio by 8 to get the number of each type of book:
7 × 8 = 56 non-fiction books
9 × 8 = 72 fiction books

Then subtract the removals and find the new total:
56 – 14 = 42 non-fiction left

72 − 10 = 62 fiction left
42 + 62 = 104 total books left
Finally, express the fiction books as a fraction of the total: 62 / 104 = 31 / 52

45) The correct answer is B. For questions about scale, divide the actual distance by the corresponding distance on the map to get the scale of the map. The actual distance between the Ferris wheel and the entrance is 350 yards, and this is represented by 8 inches on the map, so divide to get the scale: 350 ÷ 8 = 43.75. In other words, every inch on the map represents 43.75 yards. Now multiply the scale of the map by the number of inches between the entrance and the roller coaster to get the actual distance: 6.5 × 43.75 = 284.375. Finally, round to 284 yards.

46) The correct answer is A. To find the distance between two points on a graph, you need to use the distance formula:

$$d = \sqrt{(x_2 - x_1)^2 + (y_2 - y_1)^2}$$

Put in the values provided, which were $\left(4\sqrt{7}, -2\right)$ and $\left(7\sqrt{7}, 4\right)$ and which represent (x_1, y_1) and (x_2, y_2) for the formula.

$$\sqrt{(x_2 - x_1)^2 + (y_2 - y_1)^2} =$$

$$\sqrt{\left(7\sqrt{7} - 4\sqrt{7}\right)^2 + (4 - -2)^2}$$

Then expand and multiply.

$$\sqrt{\left(7\sqrt{7} - 4\sqrt{7}\right)^2 + (4 - -2)^2} =$$

$$\sqrt{\left(3\sqrt{7}\right)^2 + (6)^2} =$$

$$\sqrt{(3 \times 3)(\sqrt{7} \times \sqrt{7}) + (6 \times 6)} =$$

$$\sqrt{(9 \times 7) + 36} =$$

$$\sqrt{63 + 36}$$

Finally, simplify by finding the largest common factor that is a perfect square, which in this case is 9.

$$\sqrt{63 + 36} = \sqrt{99} = \sqrt{9 \times 11} = 3\sqrt{11}$$

47) The correct answer is D. Read the facts carefully for questions involving maps and then make conclusions based on the information provided. You may find it helpful to draw diagrams to help you answer these types of questions. For some questions, a diagram may be provided.

For questions about distance like this one, keep in mind that the locations may or may not lie on a straight line. For example, the locations could be laid out on the map like this:

Police station   ⟶   Fire station   ⟶   Hospital
                10 miles   6 miles

In the layout above, the police station would be 16 miles from the hospital.

However, the locations could also be laid out like this:

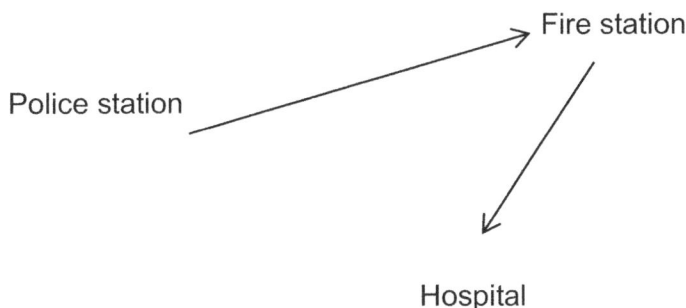

We can see that the locations will be the farthest from each other if they are laid out on a straight line as in the first example above. In other words, a person could always go to the hospital by traveling to the fire station from the police station (10 miles) and then traveling from the fire station to the hospital (6 miles). Therefore, the police station would never be more than 16 miles away from the hospital, regardless of the layout.

48) The correct answer is D. When two parallel lines are cut by a transversal (a straight line that runs through or connects both of the parallel lines), opposite angles are formed. These opposite angles are equal in measure. In the illustration, angle z and the angle that measures $2x°$ are opposite angles. Angle u and the 48° angle are also opposite angles. Because of these principles stated, angle z measures $2x°$. Remember that there are 180° degrees in total when we add up the three angles of any triangle and that two angles that form a straight line also add up to 180°.

So, we set up our equation for the triangle as follows: $180° = z° + x° + 48°$
We simplify this as shown:
$180° = z° + x° + 48°$
$180° = 2x° + x° + 48°$
$180° = 3x° + 48°$
$180° - 48° = 3x°$
$132° = 3x°$
$44° = x$

Then calculate the measurement of angle z:
$z° = 2x°$
$z° = 2 × 44°$
$z = 88$

Finally, since $y° + z°$ forms a straight line and because straight lines measure 180°, we can calculate the measurement of angle y: 180° (for the straight line) – 88° (for angle z) = 92°

49) The correct answer is D. Remember that opposite sides of a rectangle are equal in length. You may also wish to refer back to the rules on angles provided previously.

$\overline{WY}$ and $\overline{XZ}$ are opposite sides of the rectangle, and opposite sides are equal in length. The two opposite sides of a rectangle are also called corresponding sides.

50) The correct answer is C. Circle A contains these numbers: 3, 4, 5, 6, 7, 8, 9, 10, 11, 12, 13. Circle B contains these numbers: 5, 6, 7, 8, 9, 10, 11, 12, 13, 14, 15. Now look to see which numbers are included in both data sets for region C. 5, 6, 7, 8, 9, 10, 11, 12, 13 are included in both sets. So, region C contains 9 numbers.

CHSPE Math Practice Test 4

1) An online magazine business charges a $59 subscription fee for every customer who signs up during the week. This week, 14 customers signed up. How much did the business make on upfront subscription fees for these customers this week?
A) $726
B) $762
C) $826
D) $862

2) Packaging weight changes for the first three years of business were as follows. Year 1: −92 grams; Year 2: 35 grams; Year 3: −16 grams. What figure below represents the change in the packaging weight from year 1 to year 2?
A) −57
B) 57
C) 19
D) 127

3) A business's expenses for the first three years were as follows: $12,225; $43,871; and $69,423. What were the total expenses for the first three years of business?
A) $125,339
B) $125,465
C) $125,519
D) $125,528

4) A customer handed the cashier $75 to pay for the items she purchased, and the cashier gave her the correct change of $8.35. What was the total cost of the items the customer purchased?
A) $66.65
B) $66.75
C) $65.65
D) $66.55

5) Stock option investments can go up or down in value each day. Investment gains are represented as positive numbers, and investment losses are represented as negative numbers. At the end of one particular day, the gains and losses for five investments were as follows: −205, 39, −107, 18, 126. What was the total investment gain or loss for all five investments for this day?
A) 85
B) 129
C) −129
D) −192

6) An auto shop does custom paint and vinyl wrap jobs on vintage cars. An employee worked 7.5 hours each day for 2 days on a job for one customer. The customer was billed $75 per hour for the employee's work, and the employee was paid $40 per hour. How much money did the shop make for the work on this job after paying the employee's wages?
A) $262.50
B) $300.00
C) $525.00
D) $600.00

7) A liquid ingredient is stored in 5-quart containers. There are two partially-full containers, one with $4^3/_8$ quarts and another with $3^7/_8$ quarts. How many quarts are there in total in these two containers?
A) $1^1/_4$
B) 7
C) $7^1/_8$
D) $8^1/_4$

8) A small factory uses tarpaulin to make covers for farm implements. There was $12^7/_{16}$ yards of tarpaulin at the start of the day. At the end of the day, $8^9/_{16}$ yards of tarpaulin is left. Which amount below represents the amount of tarpaulin used this day in yards?
A) $2^{14}/_{16}$
B) $3^1/_8$
C) $3^7/_8$
D) $4^7/_8$

9) Abdul purchased 80 items for sale, and he has sold 0.75 of them in relation to the total purchased. How many items does he have left after making these sales?
A) 10 items
B) 20 items
C) 25 items
D) 40 items

10) A class has n students. In this class, t% of the students subscribe to digital TV packages. Which of the following represents the number of students who do not subscribe to any digital TV package?
A) $100(n - t)$
B) $(100\% - t\%) \times n$
C) $(100\% - t\%) \div n$
D) $(1 - t)n$

11) For a particular sugar-craft product, 3 parts of icing sugar must be added to every 6 parts of sugar paste. A batch of sugar-craft that has 14 parts of sugar paste is being prepared. How many parts of icing sugar should be added to this batch?
A) 3
B) 6
C) 7
D) 8

12) In a shipment of 200 televisions, 1% of the TVs are faulty. What is the ratio of non-faulty TVs to faulty TVs?
   A) 99:1
   B) 1:100
   C) 100:1
   D) 1:99

13) A retailer purchases sofas at a cost of x and sells them at four times the cost. Which of the following represents the profit on each of these sofas?
   A) x
   B) $3x$
   C) $4x$
   D) $3 - x$

14) A cell phone company sells monthly data packages. The price (P) for the data packages depends on the number of gigabytes (g) of data used. The chart below shows the prices of the data packages.
   Price in Dollars: $20 $40 $60 $80
   Speed in GB: 4   8   12   16
   Which equation represents the prices of these data packages?
   A) $P = (g - 5) \times 5$
   B) $P = (g + 5) \times 5$
   C) $P = 5 \div g$
   D) $P = g \times 5$

15) During the first nine hours of production, the following amounts of units were produced per hour: 1, 2, 3, 4, 5, 5, 8, 8, 9. Which figure below represents the mean production in units per hour for the first nine hours of production?
   A) 1
   B) 2
   C) 5
   D) 8

16) Seven orders were received yesterday for the following numbers of units: 12, 20, 3, 25, 30, 28, and 18. What was the median number of units ordered yesterday?
   A) 12
   B) 13
   C) 20
   D) 35

17) R represents rugs and P represents pillows in these equations: $2R + P = \$50$ and $R + 2P = \$40$. Darnella buys one rug and one pillow. How much does she pay in total?
   A) $10
   B) $20
   C) $30
   D) $40

18) Galvanized pipe is manufactured in 1/64 inch increments in diameter. You have selected a pipe that is 23/64 inch diameter, but have realized that it is too large for your current project. What size diameter should you try next?
A) 1/4
B) 11/32
C) 12/32
D) 13/32

19) A footwear store can purchase 325 pairs of tennis shoes from its normal supplier for $4 a pair. It can get the same 325 pairs of shoes from a second supplier for $1,250 plus 6% sales tax, or from a third supplier for $1,290. How much will the store pay to get the best deal?
A) $1,250.00
B) $1,290.00
C) $1,300.00
D) $1,367.40

20) A textile manufacturing company can buy cloth for $3 a meter from an overseas supplier. However, the cost of the cloth needs to be reported in inches for the company's financial statements. How many inches of cloth can be purchased for $3?
A) 2.54
B) 3.937
C) 39.37
D) 100

21) Your teacher has told you that your homework will count 40 percent, your midterm exam will count 25 percent, and your final exam will count 35 percent towards your grade. You scored 100 percent on your homework, 85 percent of your midterm, and 90 percent on your final exam. What percentage grade will you get for the class?
A) 91.67
B) 92.25
C) 92.75
D) 94.00

22) What is the value of | xy | when x = –10 and y = 14?
A) –140
B) 140
C) –4
D) 4

23) $(3a^2 + 4ab + 2b^2) + (7a^2 - ab - 6b^2) + (8a^2 - 5ab - 4b^2) = ?$
A) $18a^2 - 2ab + 8b^2$
B) $18a^2 + 2ab - 8b^2$
C) $18a^2 - 2ab - 8b^2$
D) $18a^2 + 2ab + 8b^2$

24) In the xy-plane, a line passes through the point (–2, 9) and has a slope of 5. Which of the following is an equation of the line?
A) y = 5x + 9
B) y = 5x – 2
C) y = –2x + 5
D) y = 5x + 19

25) Express the following number in scientific notation: 8,712
A) 8.712×10^4
B) 0.8712×10^2
C) 87.12×10^1
D) 8.712×10^3

26) The times for competitors in a race are shown in the chart below. What is the range in the scores?

Name	Time in Minutes
Anderson, B.	34.76
Carlton, R.	32.98
Denner, M.	31.21
Machelfield, S.	32.43
Zohl, A.	35.89

A) 132.51 minutes
B) 4.68 minutes
C) 33.1275 minutes
D) 31.82 minutes

27) The length of the minute hand on a circular clock is 5 inches long. What is the approximate distance traveled by the end point of the minute hand in one hour? Use 3.14 for π.
A) 314 inches
B) 25 inches
C) 31.4 inches
D) 78.5 inches

28) A cartographer needs to calculate the distance between cities in a particular area. She has measured a distance between two cities of 38 miles. What is the approximate distance between the cities in terms of kilometers?
A) 3800
B) 125
C) 61

29) In the xy-plane, a line passes through the points (2, 4) and (4, –6). Which of the following is an equation of this line?
A) y = –5x + 14
B) y = 5x + 14
C) y = –5x – 14
D) y = 5x – 14

30) The triangle in the xy-plane below will be rotated 180° clockwise about the origin and then reflected across the x-axis to produce a new triangle. The coordinates of vertex A of the original triangle are (4, 0), and vertex A' of the new triangle will correspond to vertex A of the original triangle. Which one of the following could be the coordinates of vertex A' of the new triangle?

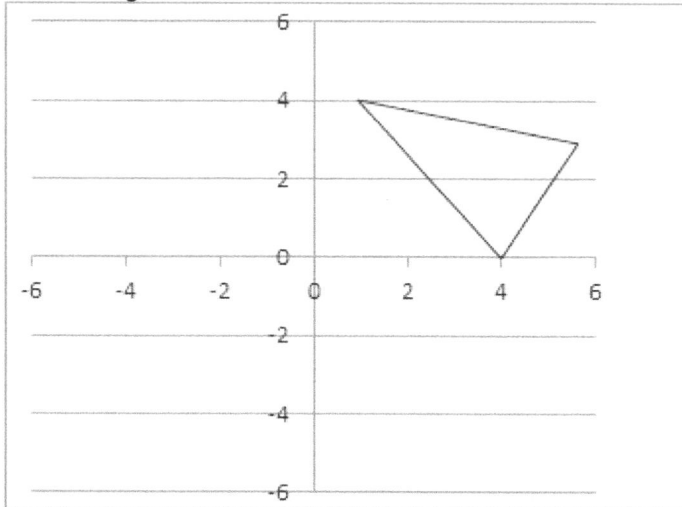

A) (−4, 0)
B) (0, −4)
C) (4, 0)
D) (0, 4)

31) $(25x)^0$
A) 0
B) 5
C) 1
D) 25

32) $4^{11} \times 4^8 = ?$
A) 16^{19}
B) 4^{19}
C) 8^{19}
D) 4^{88}

33) $\sqrt{8x^4} \cdot \sqrt{32x^6} = ?$
A) $8\sqrt{32x^{10}}$
B) $16x^{10}$
C) $16x^5$
D) $256x^{10}$

34) Angle A of a triangle measures 36°. Angles B and C have the same measurement each in degrees. What is the measurement of angle B?
A) 36°
B) 45°
C) 72°
D) 144°

35) A football field is 100 yards long and 30 yards wide. What is the area of the football field in square yards?
A) 3000
B) 1500
C) 300
D) 260

36) A small pasture has a length of 5 yards and a width of 3 yards. Barbed wire will be placed on all four sides of the outside of this pasture. How many yards of barbed wire should be ordered?
A) 15
B) 16
C) 18
D) 40

37) A circular ornament has a diameter of 12. Which formula should be used to calculate the approximate circumference of the ornament?
A) 6 × 3.14
B) 12 × 3.14
C) 24 × 3.14
D) 36 × 3.14

38) A box is manufactured to contain either laptop computers or notebook computers. When the computer systems are removed from the box, it is reused to hold other items. If the length of the box is 20 centimeters (cm), the width is 15cm, and the height is 25cm, what is the volume of the box in cubic centimeters?
A) 150
B) 300
C) 750
D) 7500

39) A production line has 6 different production stages that the product must pass through before it is completed. Each production stage lasts for 9 seconds, and the set-up time for each stage is an additional 2 seconds. The production line shift begins at 6:00 AM and a count of items produced takes place every 10 minutes, with the first count to take place at 6:10 AM. The items are counted after they are placed into a box, and there is a further 5 second packaging time for each box that is filled. How many items will have been packaged in the box when the first count is taken at 6:10 AM?
A) 0
B) 6
C) 9
D) 3

40) An individual tire-and-rim product weighs 32 pounds and 4 ounces. The product is loaded into a wooden crate, and the crate when empty weighs 60 pounds. Each individual rim weighs 19 pounds. The crate when completely full to capacity weighs 447 pounds. How many units can each crate contain?
A) 11
B) 12
C) 13
D) 14

41) The legend for a map shows that 1 inch on the map is equal to 20 miles in actual distance. There is a space of 2 and a half inches between two cities on the map. What figure below best represents the actual distance in kilometers between these two cities?
A) 31.06
B) 32.2
C) 80.5
D) 322

42) 5 boxes can be packaged in 1 and a half hours, and an extra 4 minutes per box is needed to fill out a shipping form in order to prepare the box for shipment. 14 boxes need to be packaged and prepared for shipment today. How long should it take to package all 14 boxes and prepare them for shipment?
A) 2 hours and 52 minutes
B) 4 hours and 12 minutes
C) 5 hours and 8 minutes
D) 3 hours and 8 minutes

43) A certain brand of aquarium water treatment comes in a 2-quart size container. The treatment is repackaged into two sizes of bottles for resale. An 8-ounce size bottle of the treatment and a larger 12-ounce size bottle are sold in your store. You have 3 quarts of the treatment left in stock. You want to be able to have 25 units of the 8-ounce bottles and 20 units of the 12-ounce bottles on the shelf for sale and a further 4 quarts left in stock after you have filled all of the bottles. How many containers of the treatment do you need to buy in order to fill all of the bottles and have 4 quarts left in stock?
A) 8
B) 14
C) 15
D) 16

44) A wastewater company measures the amount of wastewater usage per household in wastewater units (WWU's). During one calendar quarter, the houses on a particular street had these measurements: 682, 534, 689, 783, and 985. What is the mode of wastewater usage in WWU's for this quarter for these properties?
A) no mode
B) 451
C) 689
D) 734.6

45) Aleesha rolls a fair pair of six-sided dice. Each die has values from 1 to 6. She rolls an even number on her first roll. What is the probability that she will roll an odd number on her next roll?

A) $^1/_2$

B) $^1/_6$

C) $^2/_6$

D) $^6/_{11}$

46) Express as a logarithmic function: $6^3 = 216$
   A) $6 = \log_3 32$
   B) $3 = \log_6 216$
   C) $6 = \log_{216} 3$
   D) $216 = \log_6 3$

47) What is the domain of the following function $f(x)$?

$$f(x) = \frac{x^2}{\sqrt{x}}$$

   A) All real numbers.
   B) All negative real numbers.
   C) All positive real numbers.
   D) Cannot be determined.

48)   Which of the following equations could define $f(x)$?

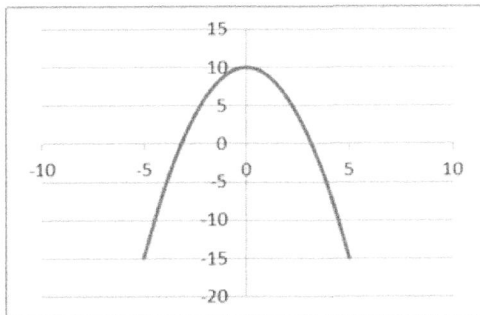

   A) $f(x) = x + 10$
   B) $f(x) = x^2 - 10$
   C) $f(x) = x^2 + 10$
   D) $f(x) = -(x^2) + 10$

49) If a = 2 and b = 5, what is the value of the following? $a\sqrt{5} \times b\sqrt{20}$

    A) 70

    B) $7\sqrt{25}$

    C) $10\sqrt{10}$

    D) 100

50) Solve for a and b if 4a – 3b = 11 and 2a + 2b = –5

    A) a = $^1/_2$ and b = –3

    B) a = 5 and b = 3

    C) a = –3 and b = $^1/_2$

    D) a = 3 and b = $^1/_3$

Answers and Explanations for CHSPE Math Practice Test 4

1) The correct answer is C. The problem states that you get a $59 subscription for every new customer, so we need to multiply the amount of the subscription fee by the number of new customers to solve: $59 × 14 = $826

2) The correct answer is D. Perform the operation as shown: 35 − (−92) = 127. Express your result as a positive number since the value has increased from year 1 to year 2.

3) The correct answer is C. The problem is asking for the total for all three years, so we add the three amounts together: $ 12,225 + $43,871 + $ 69,423= $125,519

4) The correct answer is A. Take the amount of money the customer gives the cashier and subtract the amount of the change provided to calculate the amount of the purchase: $75.00 − $8.35 = $66.65

5) The correct answer is C. Add to solve: −205 + 39 − 107 + 18 + 126 = −129

6) The correct answer is C. Step 1 – Determine the total number of hours worked: 7.5 hours per day for 2 days = 7.5 × 2 = 15 hours. Step 2 – Calculate the profit the company makes per hour. The customer was billed $75 per hour for the work, and the employee was paid $40 per hour: $75 − $40 = $35 profit per hour. Step 3 – Multiply the total number of hours by the profit per hour to solve: 15 hours × $35 profit per hour = $525

7) The correct answer is D. Step 1 – Add the whole numbers: 4 + 3 = 7. Step 2 – Add the fractions: 3/8 + 7/8 = 10/8. Step 3 – Simplify the fraction from Step 2: 10/8 = 8/8 + 2/8 = 1 + 2/8 = $1^2/_8$ = $1^1/_4$. Step 4 – Combine the results from Step 1 and Step 3 to solve the problem: 7 + $1^1/_4$ = $8^1/_4$

8) The correct answer is C. In this problem, the fraction on the second number is larger than the fraction on the first number, so we need to convert the first fraction before we start our calculation. Step 1 – Convert $12^7/_{16}$ for subtraction: $12^7/_{16}$ = $11^7/_{16}$ + 1 = $11^7/_{16}$ + $^{16}/_{16}$ = $11^{23}/_{16}$. Step 2 – There were $8^9/_{16}$ yards left, so subtract the whole numbers: 11 − 8 = 3. Step 3 – Subtract the fractions: 23/16 − 9/16 = 14/16. Step 4 – Simplify the fraction from Step 3: 14/16 = (14 ÷ 2)/(16 ÷ 2) = 7/8. Step 4 – Combine the results from Step 2 and Step 4 to get your new mixed number to solve the problem: 3 + 7/8 = $3^7/_8$

9) The correct answer is B. The problem tells us the relative number of units sold, but the question is asking for the relative number of units left. So, subtract the decimal from 1 to find the relative amount left: 1 − 0.75 = 0.25. Then multiply the total number of items at the start by this decimal number: 80 items × 0.25 = 80 × 0.25 = 20 items left

10) The correct answer is B. In our problem, if t% of the students subscribe to digital TV packages, then 100% − t% do not subscribe. In other words, since a percentage is any given number out of 100%, the percentage of students who do not subscribe is represented by this equation: (100% − t%). This equation is then multiplied by the total number of students (n) in order to determine the number of students who do not subscribe to digital TV packages: (100% − t%) × n

11) The correct answer is C. Step 1 – Set up the original proportion as a fraction. We have 3 parts of icing sugar for every 6 parts of sugar paste so our fraction is $^3/_6$. Step 2 – You can

61

simplify the fraction from the previous step because both the numerator and denominator are divisible by 3: $^3/_6 \div {}^3/_3 = {}^1/_2$. Step 3 – We need to use 14 parts of sugar paste for the current batch, so multiply this amount by the simplified fraction. $^1/_2 \times 14 = 7$

12) The correct answer is A. This problem is asking for the ratio of non-faulty televisions to the quantity of faulty televisions. You need to put the quantity of non-faulty TVs before the colon in the ratio. In this problem, 1% of the TVs are faulty. 1% × 200 = 2 faulty TVs in every 200 TVs. 200 − 2 = 198 non-faulty players. So, the ratio is 198:2. We divide each number by 2 to get the simplified ratio of 99:1.

13) The correct answer is B. The sales price of each sofa is four times the cost. The cost is expressed as *x*, so the sales price is 4*x*. The difference between the sales price of each sofa and the cost of each sofa is the profit. In this problem, the sales price is 4*x* and the cost is *x*.
Sales Price − Cost = Profit
4*x* − *x* = Profit
3*x* = Profit

14) The correct answer is D. The price of the data package is always 5 times the speed.
20 = 4 × 5
40 = 8 × 5
60 = 12 × 5
80 = 16 × 5
So, the price of the data package (represented by variable *P*) equals the speed (represented by variable *g*) times 5: *P* = *g* × 5

15) The correct answer is C. To calculate the mean, add up all of the values: 1 + 2 + 3 + 4 + 5 + 5 + 8 + 8 + 9 = 45. There are 9 numbers in the set, so we need to divide by 9: 45 ÷ 9 = 5

16) The correct answer is C. To find the median, first you have to put the numbers in the data set in the correct order from lowest to highest: 3, 12, 18, **20**, 25, 28, 30. The median is the middle number in the set, which is 20 in this question.

17) The correct answer is C. This is a systems of equations question. To solve the problem, take the second equation and isolate *R* on one side of the equation. By doing this, you define variable *R* in terms of variable *P*.
R + 2*P* = $40
R + 2*P* − 2*P* = $40 − 2*P*
R = $40 − 2*P*

Now substitute $40 − 2*P* for variable *R* in the first equation to solve for variable *P*.
2*R* + *P* = 50
2(40 − 2*P*) + *P* = 50
80 − 4*P* + *P* = 50
80 − 3*P* = 50
80 − 3*P* + 3*P* = 50 + 3*P*
80 = 50 + 3*P*
80 − 50 = 50 − 50 + 3*P*
30 = 3*P*

$30 \div 3 = 3P \div 3$
$10 = P$

So, now that we know that a pillow costs $10, we can substitute this value in one of the equations in order to find the value for the rug, which is variable R.
$2R + P = 50$
$2R + 10 = 50$
$2R + 10 - 10 = 50 - 10$
$2R = 40$
$2R \div 2 = 40 \div 2$
$R = 20$
Now solve for the customer's purchase. If the customer purchased one rug and one pillow, then she paid: $10 + $20 = $30

18) The correct answer is B. Step 1 – Subtract one increment: 23/64 – 1/64 = 22/64. Step 2 – Simplify your result: 22/64 = (22 ÷ 2)/(64 ÷ 2) = 11/32

19) The correct answer is B. Step 1 – Work out the cost for the usual supplier: 325 pairs × $4 = $1,300. Step 2 – Calculate the price for the second supplier: $1,250 + ($1,250 × .06) = $1,250 + $75 = $1,325. Step 3 – Compare to the third deal to solve: The third deal is $1,290 so this is the best deal.

20) The correct answer is C. We have a formula to convert meters to centimeters and another formula to convert inches to centimeters, so we will need to use those two formulas to solve the problem. Step 1 – Determine the measurement in centimeters: 1 meter = 100 centimeters. Step 2 – Convert the centimeters to inches. The formulas states that 1 inch = 2.54 centimeters. However, we need to use the formula in reverse because we are converting centimeters to inches. So, divide to solve: 100 ÷ 2.54 = 39.37 inches

21) The correct answer is C. This is a question on weighted mean. For a weighted mean, you need to multiply each item by its percentage and then add these results together.
Set up an equation to calculate the weighted mean:
(100 × 0.40) + (85 × 0.25) + (90 × 0.35) =
40 + 21.25 + 31.5 = 92.75

22) The correct answer is B. This is a question on absolute value. When you see an operation between two vertical lines like this, you need to make the result of the operation a positive number.
Substitute the values to solve:
$| xy | =$
$| -10 \times 14 | =$
$| -140 | =$
140

23) The correct answer is C. Combine like terms, in other words, move the terms in the equation around and put the variables with the same exponents together.
Then perform the operations to solve.
$(3a^2 + 4ab + 2b^2) + (7a^2 - ab - 6b^2) + (8a^2 - 5ab - 4b^2) =$
$3a^2 + 4ab + 2b^2 + 7a^2 - ab - 6b^2 + 8a^2 - 5ab - 4b^2 =$
$3a^2 + 7a^2 + 4ab + 2b^2 - ab - 6b^2 + 8a^2 - 5ab - 4b^2 =$

$3a^2 + 7a^2 + 8a^2 + 4ab + 2b^2 - ab - 6b^2 - 5ab - 4b^2 =$
$3a^2 + 7a^2 + 8a^2 + 4ab - ab + 2b^2 - 6b^2 - 5ab - 4b^2 =$
$3a^2 + 7a^2 + 8a^2 + 4ab - ab - 5ab + 2b^2 - 6b^2 - 4b^2 =$
$(3a^2 + 7a^2 + 8a^2) + (4ab - ab - 5ab) + (2b^2 - 6b^2 - 4b^2) =$
$18a^2 - 2ab - 8b^2$

24) The correct answer is D. We do not have the y-intercept, so we need to use the point-slope form to solve. Our coordinates are (–2, 9), so $y_1 = 9$ and $x_1 = -2$
Put these values into the formula to solve:
$y - y_1 = m(x - x_1)$
$y - 9 = 5(x - -2)$
$y - 9 = 5(x + 2)$
$y - 9 = 5x + 10$
$y - 9 + 9 = 5x + 10 + 9$
$y = 5x + 19$

25) The correct answer is D. To express a number in scientific notation: (1) The number before the times sign needs to be between 1 and 10; and (2) The number after the times sign needs to be 10 raised to an exponential power. Step 1 – Put the decimal three places to the left to get 8.712. Step 2 – Then we need to find the power of ten. Since we have moved the decimal three places, we need to use three as our exponent: 10^3. Step 3 – Combine the two above numbers for your answer: 8.712×10^3

26) The correct answer is B. The range is simply the highest number in the set minus the lowest number in the set. The lowest number is 31.21 minutes. The highest number is 35.89 minutes. The range is calculated as follows: 35.89 – 31.21 = 4.68 minutes

27) The correct answer is C. The length of the minute hand represents the radius of the circle since it extends from the middle of the circle nearly to the outside edge of the circle. The minute hand will make one complete circle in an hour.
The formula for circumference is: Circumference = 2πR
So, substitute the values to solve:
Circumference = 2πR = 2 × 3.14 × 5 = 31.4 inches

28) The correct answer is D. From the formula, we can see that 1 mile = 1.61 kilometers.
So, multiply to solve:
38 miles × 1.61 = 61.18 kilometers
We round this down to 61.

29) The correct answer is A.
Step 1 – Determine the slope. The formula for slope is:
$^{rise}/_{run} = {^{y_2 - y_1}}/_{x2 - x1}$
Substitute the values for the coordinates (2, 4) and (4, –6) to calculate the slope:
$^{-6 - 4}/_{4 - 2}$
$^{-10}/_2 = -5$
Step 2 – Determine the y-intercept. You can use the slope-intercept formula to find the y-intercept. The slope-intercept formula is: $y_2 - y_1 = m(x_2 - x_1)$. Substitute the slope value found in place of "m". Also choose one of the two points to substitute in place of x_2 and y_2.

We will use the point (2, 4) in our calculation:
$y_2 - y_1 = m(x_2 - x_1) =$
$4 - y_1 = -5(2 - x_1)$
To find the y-intercept, plug 0 in for x_1 and solve:
$4 - y_1 = -5(2 - 0) =$
$4 - y_1 = -5(2) =$
$4 - y_1 = -10 =$
$4 - 4 - y_1 = -10 - 4 =$
$-y_1 = -14$
$y_1 = 14$
Step 3 – Determine the equation of the line in the form: y = mx + b, where m is slope and b is the y-intercept. Substitute the values from the two previous steps to solve.
$y = mx + b =$
$y = -5x + 14$

30) The correct answer is A. The rule to apply for questions like this one is that when a figure is rotated 180 degrees clockwise about the origin, (x, y) becomes (–x, –y). When the triangle is rotated 180° clockwise about the origin, which is point (0, 0), the new triangle is placed in the lower left quadrant, and the coordinates (4, 0) are translated to (–4, 0) in the new triangle. Then after the new triangle is reflected, or flipped, across the x-axis, the new triangle is placed in the upper left quadrant and point (–4, 0) remains at point (–4, 0).

31) The correct answer is C. Any non-zero number to the power of zero is equal to 1.

32) The correct answer is B. $4^{11} \times 4^8 = 4^{(11 + 8)} = 4^{19}$

33) The correct answer is C. Perform the operation on the radicals and then simplify.
$$\sqrt{8x^4} \cdot \sqrt{32x^6} = \sqrt{8x^4 \times 32x^6} = \sqrt{256x^{10}} = \sqrt{16 \times 16 \times x^5 \times x^5} = 16x^5$$

34) The correct answer is C. The sum of all three angles inside a triangle is always 180 degrees. So, we need to deduct the degrees given from 180° to find out the total degrees of the two other angles: 180° – 36° = 144°. Now divide this result by two in order to determine the degrees for each angle: 144° ÷ 2 = 72°

35) The correct answer is A. The area of a rectangle is equal to its length times its width. This football field is 30 yards wide and 100 yards long, so we can substitute the values into the appropriate formula.
rectangle area = width × length
rectangle area = 30 × 100
rectangle area = 3000

36) The correct answer is B. You are being asked about the distance around the outside, so you need to calculate the perimeter, Write out the formula: (length × 2) + (width × 2). Then substitute the values: (5 × 2) + (3 × 2) = 10 + 6 = 16

37) The correct answer is B. Substitute the value of the diameter into the formula to solve.
circumference ≈ diameter × 3.14
circumference ≈ 12 × 3.14

38) The correct answer is D. To calculate the volume of a box, you need the formula for a rectangular solid: volume = base × width × height. Now substitute the values from the problem into the formula: volume = 20 × 15 × 25 = 7500

39) The correct answer is C. Step 1 – Determine the number of seconds that have passed from 6:00 AM to 6:10 AM. 10 minutes × 60 seconds per minute = 600 seconds production time. Step 2 – Subtract the packaging time. 600 seconds – 5 seconds packaging per box = 595 seconds available for production. Step 3 – Determine the production time per unit: (9 seconds production time + 2 seconds set-up time) × 6 stages = 11 seconds × 6 = 66 seconds per unit. Step 4 – Divide the available production time by the time per unit to determine how many items can be produced. 595 seconds ÷ 66 seconds = 9.015 units, which we round down to 9.

40) The correct answer is B. Step 1 – Find the total product weight, excluding the weight of the crate. 447 pounds – 60 pounds = 387 pounds. Step 2 – Convert the total product weight to ounces. 387 pounds × 16 ounces per pound = 6,192 ounces of total product weight. Step 3 – Convert the weight of each unit to ounces: 32 pounds and 4 ounces = (32 × 16) + 4 = 512 + 4 = 516 ounces each. Step 4 – Divide to solve: 6,192 ÷ 516 = 12 units

41) The correct answer is C. Step 1 – Determine the actual distance between the two cities in miles. 1 inch on the map = 20 miles, so 2.5 inches × 20 = 50 miles actual distance. Step 2 – Convert the result from Step 1 to kilometers. 1 mile = 1.61 kilometers, so 50 miles × 1.61 = 80.5 kilometers.

42) The correct answer is C. Step 1 – Determine the rate for the packaging: 1.5 hours ÷ 5 boxes = 90 minutes ÷ 5 boxes = 18 minutes per box. Step 2 – Add 4 extra minutes per box to the rate to account for the time to fill in the shipping form. 18 + 4 = 22 minutes per box needed in total. Step 3 – Calculate the time needed to package all 14 boxes and prepare them for shipment: 22 minutes × 14 = 308 minutes = 5 hours and 8 minutes

43) The correct answer is A. Step 1 – Calculate the number of ounces needed to fill the small bottles: 25 bottles × 8 ounces each = 200 ounces. Step 2 – Calculate the number of ounces needed to fill the large bottles: 20 bottles × 12 ounces each = 240 ounces. Step 3 – Add the ounces needed for the bottles and convert to quarts. There are 8 ounces in a cup, and there are 4 cups in a quart, so there are 32 ounces in a quart: 200 ounces + 240 ounces = 440 ounces ÷ 32 ounces in a quart = 13.75 quarts, which we round up to 14 quarts. Step 4 – Add the amount needed for the bottles to the amount required for stock: 14 quarts + 4 quarts = 18 quarts. Step 5 – Subtract the beginning stock from the total amount needed. 18 – 3 = 15 more quarts needed. The treatment is sold in 2-quart containers, so our result needs to be a multiple of 2, so we round up to 16 quarts, which equals 8 containers.

44) The correct answer is A. If no number is duplicated, then we say that the data set has no mode.

45) The correct answer is A. The outcome of an earlier roll does not affect the outcome of the next roll. When rolling a pair of dice, the possibility of an odd number is always $1/2$, just as the possibility of an even number is always $1/2$.

We can prove this mathematically by looking at the possible outcomes:

1,1 1,2 1,3 1,4 1,5 1,6
2,1 2,2 2,3 2,4 2,5 2,6
3,1 3,2 3,3 3,4 3,5 3,6
4,1 4,2 4,3 4,4 4,5 4,6
5,1 5,2 5,3 5,4 5,5 5,6
6,1 6,2 6,3 6,4 6,5 6,6

The odd number combinations are highlighted:

1,1 **1,2** 1,3 **1,4** 1,5 **1,6**
2,1 2,2 **2,3** 2,4 **2,5** 2,6
3,1 **3,2** 3,3 **3,4** 3,5 **3,6**
4,1 4,2 **4,3** 4,4 **4,5** 4,6
5,1 **5,2** 5,3 **5,4** 5,5 **5,6**
6,1 6,2 **6,3** 6,4 **6,5** 6,6

So, we can see that an odd number will be rolled half of the time.

46) The correct answer is B. $y^x = Z$ is the same as $x = \log_y Z$. So, $6^3 = 216$ is the same as $3 = \log_6 216$.

47) The correct answer is C. The domain of a function is all possible x values for the function. You need to avoid any mathematical operations that do not have real number solutions, such as dividing by a zero or finding the square root of a negative number. In the function in this problem, we have a square root in the denominator of the function. Negative numbers do not have real number square roots. Since we cannot use a negative value for x, the domain is all positive real numbers.

48) The correct answer is D. The graph is of a quadratic, so the equation must have a variable raised to the power of 2. So, Answer A is incorrect. The parabola is downward facing, so the leading coefficient must be negative. Answer choice D meets this criterion, but answers B and C do not. Further, we can identify points (0, 10) and (5, –15) from the graph. So, we can check the answer as follows:
$f(x) = -(x^2) + 10$
$f(x) = -(0^2) + 10 = 10$
$f(x) = -(x^2) + 10$
$f(x) = -(5^2) + 10 = -25 + 10 = -15$
Since the coordinates on the graph satisfy equation D, it is the correct answer.

49) The correct answer is B. To solve problems like this, multiply the numbers inside the radical signs. Also multiply the numbers or variables in front of the radical signs:
$a\sqrt{5} \times b\sqrt{20} = (a \times b)\sqrt{5 \times 20} = ab\sqrt{100}$
Then simplify:
$ab\sqrt{100} = ab\sqrt{10 \times 10} = 10ab$
Then substitute the values for a and b to solve:
a = 2 and b = 5
10ab = 10 × 2 × 5 = 100

67

50) The correct answer is A.
Step 1: Label the equations as equations 1 and 2.
(1) $4a - 3b = 11$
(2) $2a + 2b = -5$
Step 2: Isolate one of the variables. We will divide equation 2 by 2 to isolate variable a. Divide each term by 2.
$2a + 2b = -5$
$(2a \div 2) + (2b \div 2) = (-5 \div 2)$
$a + b = -5/2$
$a + b - b = -5/2 - b$
$a = -5/2 - b$
Step 3: Into equation 1, substitute the value of the isolated variable. We have just determined that $a = -5/2 - b$.
$4a - 3b = 11$
$[4 \times (-5/2 - b)] - 3b = 11$
Step 4: Perform the multiplication
$[4 \times (-5/2 - b)] - 3b = 11$
$(4 \times -5/2) - (4 \times b) - 3b = 11$
$-{}^{20}/_2 - 4b - 3b = 11$
Step 5: Simplify and perform inverse operations to solve for b
$-{}^{20}/_2 - 4b - 3b = 11$
$-10 - 4b - 3b = 11$
$-10 - 7b = 11$
$-10 + 10 - 7b = 11 + 10$
$-7b = 11 + 10$
$-7b = 21$
$-7b \div -7 = 21 \div -7$
$b = -3$
Step 6: Substitute the value of b to solve for a.
$2a + 2b = -5$
$2a + (2 \times -3) = -5$
$2a - 6 = -5$
$2a - 6 + 6 = -5 + 6$
$2a = -5 + 6$
$2a = 1$
$2a \div 2 = 1 \div 2$
$a = {}^1/_2$

1) An art and craft store received $7,375 for sales of a certain type of scrapbook this year. If these scrapbooks were sold for $59 each, how many of them were sold this year?
   A) 135
   B) 125
   C) 120
   D) 75

2) The increases and decreases this week for the sales of five products in units were as follows: 52, −14, 37, −28, 61? What was the total increase or decrease in units for these products for the week?
   A) −108
   B) 60
   C) 78
   D) 108

3) $^6/_{25}$ of the inventory has been sold this month. Approximately what percentage of the inventory has been sold?
   A) 0.24%
   B) 2.40%
   C) 24.0%
   D) 4.167%

4) The change to monthly cash flow is reported as a decimal figure, which is calculated by dividing the net change in cash flow into the previous month's cash flow. Last month, the change to cash flow was 0.40. What percentage best represents the change to cash flow for last month?
   A) 0.40%
   B) 4.00%
   C) 40.0%
   D) 400%

5) The temperature on Saturday was 62°F at 5:00 PM and 38°F at 11:00 PM. If the temperature fell at a constant rate on Saturday, what was the temperature at 9:00 PM?
   A) 58°F
   B) 54°F
   C) 50°F
   D) 46°F

6) Hot dogs sell for $2.50 each, and hamburgers sell for $4 each. A family went out to eat and bought 3 hamburgers. They also bought hot dogs. The total cost of their food was $22. How many hot dogs did they buy?
   A) 2
   B) 3
   C) 4
   D) 5

7) A carpenter needs to varnish 8 identical sets of kitchen cupboard doors, each of which has a surface area of 2000 square feet. If one container of varnish covers 900 square feet, what is the fewest number of containers of varnish that must be purchased to complete all 8 sets of doors?
A) 3
B) 17
C) 18
D) 19

8) Jack 3.6 miles in 45 minutes. What was his average running speed in miles per hour?
A) 4.8
B) 4.6
C) 4.2
D) 2.7

9) The price of a certain coat is reduced from $60 to $45 in a clearance sale. By what percent is the price of the coat reduced?
A) 15%
B) 20%
C) 25%
D) 33%

10) The ratio of teenagers to adults attending a weekend retreat was 6 to 7. If the total number of teenagers and adults in the class was 117, how many teenagers were in the class?
A) 48
B) 54
C) 56
D) 58

11) Members of a weight loss group report their individual weight loss to their group leader every week. During the week, the following amounts in pounds were reported: 1, 1, 3, 2, 4, 3, 1, 2, and 1. What is the mean of the weight loss for the group?
A) 1 pound
B) 2 pounds
C) 3 pounds
D) 4 pounds

12) A family has 5 children. The ages of 5 siblings are: 2, 5, 7, 12, and x. If the mean age of the 5 siblings is 8 years old, what is the age (x) of the 5th sibling?
A) 8
B) 10
C) 12
D) 14

13) Work-motion scores for one employee for each day of the week were as follows: 8.19, 7.59, 8.25, 7.35, and 9.10. What is the median of this employee's scores?
A) 7.59
B) 8.19

C) 8.25
D) 8.096

14) The relationship between the total number of chicken sandwiches a customer can buy and the total price for each order is shown below. If a customer takes the deal that has the lowest price per sandwich, what will the customer pay per sandwich?
2 chicken sandwiches for $17.50
4 chicken sandwiches for $34.40
8 chicken sandwiches for $68.00
A) $4.00
B) $8.00
C) $8.50
D) $9.50

15) A restaurant sold 15 beef dinners, 10 pork dinners, and 5 chicken dinners one day. Beef dinners sell for $10 each; pork dinners sell for $12, and the total sales of all three types of dinners for that day was $310. What price is charged for 1 chicken dinner?
A) $5
B) $8
C) $9
D) $10

16) Shanika works as a car salesperson. She earns $1,000 a month in basic pay, plus $390 for each car she sells. If she wants to earn at least $4,000 this month, what is the minimum number of cars that she must sell this month?
A) 6
B) 7
C) 8
D) 9

17) A rocket traveled 780 miles in 2 hours at a constant speed. How many miles does this rocket travel in 40 minutes?
A) 120
B) 180
C) 200
D) 260

18) A horse ran 12 furlongs in 2 minutes and 48 seconds. Assuming that the same amount of time was spent on each furlong, how many seconds does it take the horse to run one furlong?
A) 0.014 seconds
B) 0.14 seconds
C) 1.40 seconds
D) 14 seconds

19) A report states that 30 out of every 100 television viewers in Newtown watch TV for more than 25 hours her week. If there are 3,200 television viewers in Newtown, how many television viewers in Newtown watch TV for more than 25 hours per week?
A) 320
B) 750

C) 960
D) 1,067

20) An item costs $22 each if the customer collects it in person from the store, and an extra $3 for postage and handling is charged per item if the customer wants the item sent by courier. This week, 32 customers purchased this item and requested that the item be sent by courier. How much money in total did the store make on the items sold to these 32 customers?
A) $800
B) $704
C) $575
D) $96

21) $107^3/_8$ yards of adhesive plastic is needed to complete one work order and $96^1/_8$ yards of adhesive plastic is needed for another work order. How many yards of adhesive plastic is needed in total in order to complete both of these work orders?
A) $193^1/_8$
B) $203^1/_2$
C) $193^1/_4$
D) $203^1/_4$

22) A vat contains 163.75 units of red colorant, 107.50 units of blue colorant, 91.25 units of yellow colorant, and 10.30 units of black colorant. Which of the following represents, in terms of units, how full the vat is after these 4 colorants have been placed in it?
A) 362.50
B) 371.50
C) 372.80
D) 373.50

23) A customer who owns a small hotel has ordered 10 new quilts. Each quilt requires 2 yards of red fabric for the front, 1 yard of blue fabric for the front, and a further 3 yards of blue fabric for the back. The quilts need to have an embellishment in gold, and a total amount of 12 yards of gold fabric is needed to make the embellishments for all 10 quilts. Each quilt also has edging in white, and half a yard of white material is needed for the edging for each quilt. How many yards of fabric in total will be needed to complete this order?
A) 7.7
B) 77
C) 3.85
D) 38.5

24) Fence panels are going to be placed along one side of a field. Each panel is 8 feet 6 inches long. 11 panels are needed to cover the entire side of the field. How long is the field?
A) 60 feet 6 inches
B) 72 feet 8 inches
C) 93 feet 6 inches
D) 102 feet 8 inches

25) The area of a square floor is 64 square units. The floor needs to be covered entirely with tiles. Each floor tile is 4 square units. How many tiles are needed to cover the floor?
   A) 8
   B) 12
   C) 16
   D) 24

26) The base of a cylinder is at a right angle to its sides. The radius of the base of the cylinder measures 5 centimeters. The height of the cylinder is 10 centimeters. What is the volume of this container in cubic centimeters?
   A) 785
   B) 157
   C) 78.5
   D) 31.4

27) Cone A has a base radius of 9 and a height of 18. Cone B has a base radius of 3 and a height of 6. Which number below expresses the ratio of the volume of Cone A to Cone B?
   A) $^{27}/_1$
   B) $^1/_{27}$
   C) $^3/_1$
   D) $^1/_6$

28) 500 units of a particular item can be purchased for 72 cents each from one supplier or from a different supplier for $350 for all 500 units. Sales tax of 5.5% is to be added to either purchase. What is the best total price for the items, including tax?
   A) $350.00
   B) $360.00
   C) $369.25
   D) $379.80

29) Seven members of a support group are trying to gain weight. So far, the weight gain in kilograms for each of the seven members of the group is: 12, 15, 3, 7, 21, 14, and 12. What is the range of the amount of weight gain for this support group?
   A) 18
   B) 12
   C) 14
   D) 7

30) Looking at our seven group members from the question above, what is the mode?
   A) 18
   B) 12
   C) 14
   D) 7

31) If 5a + 3b = c, then a = ?
   A) $^{c-5}/_{3b}$
   B) $^{c-3b}/_5$
   C) $^{3b}/_{5+c}$
   D) $^5/_{c-3b}$

32) A line in the xy-plane passes through point Q, which has the coordinates (5, –3), and point R, which has the coordinates (–2, 6). The line is going to be shifted 3 units to the right and 5 units down. What will the coordinates of point Q be after the shift?
A) (0, 0)
B) (0, –8)
C) (8, –8)
D) (–8, 8)

33) Which of the following is equivalent to $2ab^2(3ab^3 + 2b)$?
A) $6a^2b^5 + 4ab^3$
B) $6a^2b^6 + 4ab^3$
C) $6a^2b^5 + 4ab^2$
D) $6a^2b^6 + 4ab^3$

34) A bag in a grocery store contains 10 pink apples, 20 green apples, and 35 red apples. Customers are given an apple from the bag at random. The first customer received a pink apple, the second customer received a green apple, and the third customer received a red apple. What is the probability that the next customer will receive a green apple? Note that apples are eaten and therefore not placed back into the bag once they have been drawn.
A) $^{20}/_{62}$
B) $^{20}/_{65}$
C) $^{19}/_{62}$
D) $^{19}/_{65}$

35) For a particular sugar-craft product, 3 parts of icing sugar must be added to every 6 parts of sugar paste. A batch of sugar-craft that has 14 parts of sugar paste is being prepared. How many parts of icing sugar should be added to this batch?
A) 3
B) 6
C) 7
D) 8

36) If 8x is between 3 and 4, which of the following could be the value of x?
A) $^2/_3$
B) $^2/_5$
C) $^1/_8$
D) $^3/_5$

37) 4 out of every 5 employee-satisfaction questionnaires have been completed and returned. If a company has 250 total employees, and every employee must complete and return the questionnaire, how many questionnaires have not been completed and returned?
A) 4
B) 5
C) 50
D) 200

38) The chart below summarizes tax money spent on municipal services for Newtown last year:

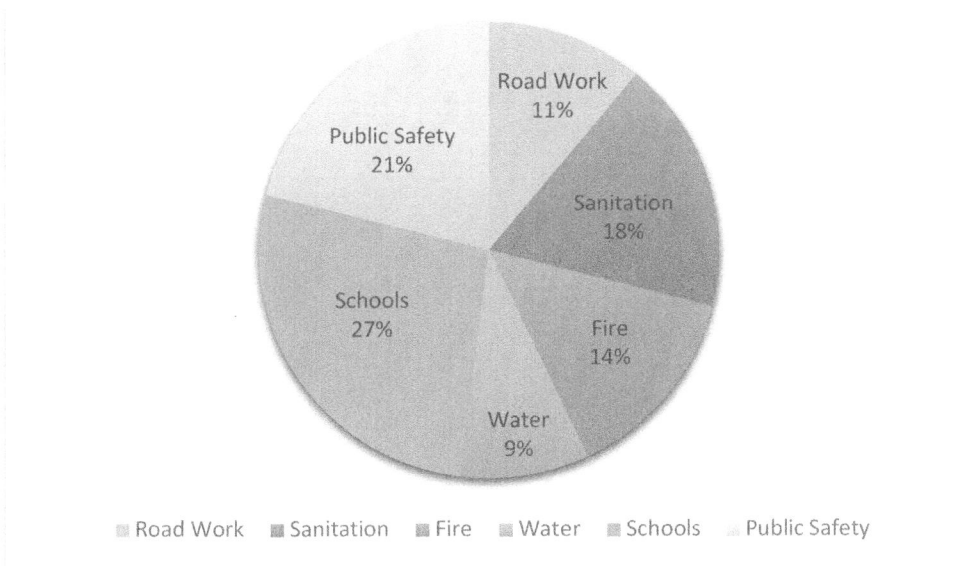

If $5,275,300 in total tax money was spent on all municipal services, how much was spent on schools?
A) $474,777
B) $580,283
C) $1,107,813
D) $1,424,331

39) Given sets P, Q, and R below, which of the following represents $(P \cap Q) \cap R$?
P = {3, 6, 9, 12, 15}
Q = {1, 3, 5, 7, 9, 11}
R = {0, 1, 9, 81}
A) The set is empty.
B) {9}
C) {3, 9}
D) {0, 1, 9, 81}

40) Which of the following expressions is equivalent to:
$15xy - 20x^2y - 40x^2y^2$?
A) $5xy(3 - 4x - 8xy)$
B) $4xy(4 - 8x - 16xy)$
C) $5x^2y(3 - 4 - 8y)$
D) $5xy(3 - 4x + 8xy)$

41) A pharmacist owns a local drug store. Last week, she filled 250 prescriptions in 40 hours. Assuming that each prescription takes the same amount of time, how many minutes should it take her to fill a single prescription?
A) 9.6 minutes
B) 6.25 minutes
C) 3.75 minutes
D) 0.16 minutes

42) What is the area in square units of the triangle shown below?

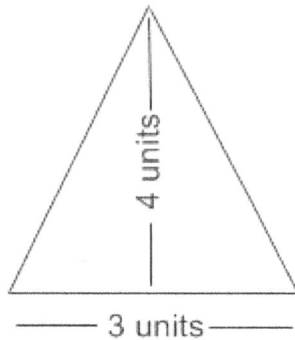

A) 3 square units
B) 6 square units
C) 12 square units
D) 24 square units

43) Consider the following data set. What is the mode?
5, 4, 6, 11, 12, 14, 15, 7, 8, 10, 13, 9
A) 9
B) 9.5
C) 10
D) No mode

44) The cities Bellevue, Poplar Falls, and Wayward Pines all lie on state highway A. If you start at Bellevue and travel to Poplar Falls, the distance is 1,500 meters. Wayward Pines is a further 1,200 meters past Poplar Falls. What is the distance between Bellevue and Poplar Falls in millimeters?
A) 2,700,000 millimeters
B) 2.7 millimeters
C) 0.27 millimeters
D) 2,700 millimeters

45) $a \times b^0 = ?$
A) 0
B) ab
C) $^a/_b$
D) a

46) A line in the xy-plane is represented by the equation: $y = 2x + 5$. Which of the following could be a point on this line?
A) (1, 7)
B) (2, 5)
C) (5, 0)
D) (7, 1)

47) A cylinder has a volume of 640π cubic inches. If the height of the cylinder is 10 inches, what is the area of the base of the cylinder?
A) 8π square inches
B) 16π square inches
C) 64π square inches
D) 100π square inches

48) $12 + 15 - 300 \div 100 \times 3 - 180 + 9 = ?$
A) −179.19
B) −179.91
C) −145
D) −153

49) $(5ab^5)(-6ab^3) = ?$
A) $-a^2b^8$
B) $-30a^2b^{15}$
C) $-30a^2b^8$
D) $-a^2b^{15}$

50) During a particular day, a dentist records the number of existing fillings that his patients have when he examines them:
1, 0, 6, 4, 3, 2, 3, 0, 1, 7, 2, 4, 0, 2, 3, 2, 5, 1, 2, 3

What is the median number of fillings for these patients?
A) 7
B) 2.55
C) 2
D) 2.5

Answers and Explanations for CHSPE Math Practice Test 5

1) The correct answer is B. Divide the total amount by the sales price per unit to solve: $7,375 ÷ $59 = 125 units sold

2) The correct answer is D. Add the increases and subtract the decreases: 52 – 14 + 37 – 28 + 61 = 108

3) The correct answer is C. Divide and then express the result as a percentage. Step 1 – Treat the line in the fraction as the division symbol: 6/25 = 6 ÷ 25 = 0.24. Step 2 – To express the result from Step 1 as a percentage, move the decimal point two places to the right and add the percent sign: 0.24 = 24.0%

4) The correct answer is C. Move the decimal point two places to the right and add the percent sign: 0.40 = 40.0%

5) The correct answer is D. First of all, determine the temperature difference during the entire time period: 62 – 38 = 24 degrees less. Then calculate how much time has passed. From 5:00 PM to 11:00 PM, 6 hours have passed. Next, divide the temperature difference by the amount of time that has passed to get the temperature change per hour: 24 degrees ÷ 6 hours = 4 degrees less per hour. To calculate the temperature at the stated time, you need to calculate the time difference. From 5:00 PM to 9:00 PM, 4 hours have passed. So, the temperature difference during the stated time is 4 hours × 4 degrees per hour = 16 degrees less. Finally, deduct this from the beginning temperature to get your final answer: 62°F – 16°F = 46°F

6) The correct answer is C. The number of hot dogs is *D* and the number of hamburgers is *H*. The equation to express the problem is: (*D* × $2.50) + (*H* × $4) = $22. We know that the number of hamburgers is 3, so put that in the equation and solve it.
(*D* × $2.50) + (*H* × $4) = $22
(*D* × $2.50) + (3 × $4) = $22
(*D* × $2.50) + 12 = $22
(*D* × $2.50) + 12 – 12 = $22 – 12
(*D* × $2.50) = $10
$2.50*D* = $10
$2.50*D* ÷ $2.50 = $10 ÷ $2.50
D = 4

7) The correct answer is C. For your first step, determine how many square feet there are in total: 2000 square per set × 8 sets = 16,000 square feet in total. Then you need to divide by the coverage rate: 16,000 square feet to cover ÷ 900 square feet coverage per container = 17.77 containers needed. It is not possible to purchase a partial container of varnish, so 17.77 is rounded up to 18 containers of varnish.

8) The correct answer is A. First, express the time as a fraction: 45 minutes = ¾ hour. Then divide the distance traveled by the time in order to get the speed in miles per hour. Remember that in order to divide by a fraction, you need to invert the fraction, and then multiply. 3.6 miles ÷ ³/₄ = 3.6 × ⁴/₃ = (3.6 × 4) ÷ 3 = 14.4 ÷ 3 = 4.8 miles per hour

9) The correct answer is C. Step 1 – Determine the dollar amount of the reduction or discount: $60 original price – $45 sale price = $15 discount. Step 2 – Then divide the discount by the original price to get the percentage of the discount: $15 ÷ $60 = 0.25 = 25%

10) The correct answer is B. For your first step, add the subsets of the ratio together: 6 + 7 = 13. Then divide this into the total: 117 ÷ 13 = 9. Finally, multiply the result from the previous step by the subset of teenagers from the original ratio: 6 × 9 = 54 teenagers in the class

11) The correct answer is B. First add up all of the values: 1 + 1 + 3 + 2 + 4 + 3 + 1 + 2 + 1 = 18 There are nine values, so we divide to get the mean: 18 ÷ 9 = 2

12) The correct answer is D. Set up your equation to calculate the average, using x for the age of the 5th sibling:
$(2 + 5 + 7 + 12 + x) ÷ 5 = 8$
$(2 + 5 + 7 + 12 + x) ÷ 5 × 5 = 8 × 5$
$(2 + 5 + 7 + 12 + x) = 40$
$26 + x = 40$
$26 – 26 + x = 40 – 26$
$x = 14$

13) The correct answer is B. The problem provides the number set: 8.19, 7.59, 8.25, 7.35, 9.10. First of all, put the numbers in ascending order: 7.35, 7.59, 8.19, 8.25, 9.10. Then find the one that is in the middle: 7.35, 7.59, **8.19**, 8.25, 9.10

14) The correct answer is C. For 2 sandwiches, the total price is $17.50, so each sandwich in this deal sells for $8.75: $17.50 total price ÷ 2 sandwiches = $8.75 each. For 4 sandwiches, the total price is $34.40, so each sandwich in this deal sells for $8.60: $34.40 total price ÷ 4 sandwiches = $8.60 each. For 8 sandwiches, the total price is $68, so each sandwich in this deal sells for $8.50: $68 total price ÷ 8 sandwiches = $8.50 each. So, the best price per sandwich is $8.50.

15) The correct answer is B. First, determine the total sales value of the beef and pork dinners based on the prices stated in the problem: (15 beef dinners × $10 each) + (10 pork dinners × $12 each) = $150 + $120 = $270. The remaining amount is allocable to the chicken dinners: Total sales of $310 – $270 = $40 worth of chicken dinners. The problems states that 5 chicken dinners were sold. We calculate the price of the chicken dinners as follows: $40 worth of chicken dinners ÷ 5 chicken dinners sold = $8 per chicken dinners

16) The correct answer is C. Shanika wants to earn $4,000 this month. She gets the $1,000 basic pay regardless of the number of cars she sells, so we need to subtract that from the total first: $4,000 – $1,000 = $3,000. She gets $390 for each car she sells, so we need to divide that into the remaining $3,000: $3,000 to earn ÷ $390 per car = 7.69 cars to sell. Since it is not possible to sell a part of a car, we need to round up to 8 cars.

17) The correct answer is D. First, we can perform division to determine that the rocket travels 6.5 miles per minute: 780 miles ÷ 120 minutes = 6.5 miles per minute. Since the rocket travels at a constant speed, we multiply this amount by 40 minutes to solve: 6.5 miles per minute × 40 minutes = 260 miles

18) The correct answer is D. Step 1 – Determine the amount of time in seconds: 2 minutes and 48 seconds = (2 minutes × 60 seconds per minute) + 48 seconds = 120 seconds + 48 seconds = 168 seconds. Step 2 – Divide by the number of furlongs to find the rate: 168 seconds ÷ 12 furlongs = 14 seconds per furlong

19) The correct answer is C. Step 1 – Take the total number of viewers and divide this by the 100 viewers in the original ratio: 3200 ÷ 100 = 32. Step 2 – Take the result from Step 1 and multiply by the amount in the subset to solve: 32 × 30 = 960

20) The correct answer is A. Step 1 – Add the charge for postage and handling to the original price per item: $22 + $3 = $25. Step 2 – Take the result from Step 1 and multiply by the number of items sold: $25 × 32 = $800

21) The correct answer is B. Step 1 – Add the whole numbers: 107 + 96 = 203. Step 2 – Add the fractions: 3/8 + 1/8 = 4/8 = 1/2. Step 3 – Combine the results from Step 1 and Step 2 to get your new mixed number to solve the problem: 203 + 1/2 = $203^1/_2$

22) The correct answer is C. Add the four figures together to solve:
163.75 + 107.50 + 91.25 + 10.30 = 372.80

23) The correct answer is B. Step 1 – Find the amount of material needed for each quilt: 2 yards red, 4 yards blue, 1.2 yards gold (12 ÷ 10 = 1.2), and 0.5 yards white = 2 + 4 + 1.2 + 0.5 = 7.7 yards each. Step 2 – Multiply the total number of quilts by the number of yards per quilt to solve: 10 × 7.7 = 77

24) The correct answer is C. Each panel is 8 feet 6 inches long, and you need 11 panels to cover the entire side of the field. So, we need to multiply 8 feet 6 inches by 11. Step 1 – 8 feet × 11 = 88 feet. Step 2 – 6 inches × 11 = 66 inches. Step 3 – Now simplify the result. There are 12 inches in a foot, so we need to determine how many feet and inches there are in 66 inches. 66 inches ÷ 12 = 5 feet 6 inches. Step 4 – Add the two results together. 88 feet + 5 feet 6 inches = 93 feet 6 inches.

25) The correct answer is C. Since we are dealing with a square, all four sides of the floor are equal to each other. The tiles are also square, so they also have equal sides. Therefore, we can simply divide to get the answer: 64 ÷ 4 = 16

26) The correct answer is A. The volume of a cylinder is calculated as follows: volume ≈ 3.14 × $(radius)^2$ × height ≈ 3.14 × $(5)^2$ × 10 ≈ 785

27) The correct answer is A. First, we need to calculate the volume of cone A: (3.14 × 9^2 × 18) ÷ 3 = 1526.04. Then, we need to calculate the volume of Cone B: (3.14 × 3^2 × 6) ÷ 3 = 56.52. Then divide to get the ratio: 1526.04 ÷ 56.52 = 27. So, we can express the ratio as: $^{27}/_1$

28) The correct answer is C. Step 1 – Determine the cost from the first supplier: 500 × 0.72 = $360.00. The tax on this will be $360.00 × 5.5% = $19.80. Then add the tax to the cost to get the total: $360.00 + $19.80 = $379.80. Step 2 – Determine the total cost from the second supplier: $350 cost + ($350 × 0.055 tax) = $350 + 19.25 = $369.25. So, you will get the better deal from the second supplier at $369.25.

29) The correct answer is A. The range is the highest amount minus the lowest amount:
21 − 3 = 18

30) The correct answer is B. Two members have lost 12 kilograms, and all of the other amounts occur only one time each. So, 12 is the mode.

31) The correct answer is B.
Isolate a to solve:
5a + 3b = c
5a + 3b − 3b = c − 3b
5a = c − 3b
5 × a = c − 3b
5 ÷ 5 × a = c − 3b ÷ 5
a = c − 3b ÷ 5
$a = {}^{c\,-\,3b}/_5$

32) The correct answer is C. Point Q is (5, −3) at the start. The line is going to be shifted 3 units to the right (so we need to add 3 to the x coordinate) and 5 units down (so we need to subtract 5 from the y coordinate).
x coordinate after shift: 5 + 3 = 8
y coordinate after shift: −3 − 5 = −8
So, the new position of point Q will be (8, −8).

33) The correct answer is A. Multiply the integers, but add the exponents. Remember that any variable times itself is equal to that variable squared. For example, $a \times a = a^2$.
$2ab^2(3ab^3 + 2b) = (2ab^2 \times 3ab^3) + (2ab^2 \times 2b) = 6a^2b^5 + 4ab^3$

34) The correct answer is C.
Find the total of all of the apples at the start:
10 + 20 + 35 = 65
Determine how many apples are left in the bag. 3 apples have been handed out, so subtract that from the previous result:
65 − 3 = 62
Probability is a fraction, and the number above will be our denominator.
We want to know the chance of the next customer getting a green apple, so determine the number of green apples remaining:
20 − 1 = 19
Put the number of remaining green apples in the numerator to solve:
$^{19}/_{62}$

35) The correct answer is C. Step 1 − Set up the original proportion as a fraction. We have 3 parts of icing sugar for every 6 parts of sugar paste so our fraction is $^3/_6$. Step 2 − You can simplify the fraction from the previous step because both the numerator and denominator are divisible by 3: $^3/_6 \div ^3/_3 = ^1/_2$. Step 3 − We need to use 14 parts of sugar paste for the current batch, so multiply this amount by the simplified fraction: $^1/_2 \times 14 = 7$

36) The correct answer is B. The question states that 8x is between 3 and 4, so divide 3 and 4 into 8 to find the range of the values for x. In doing so, we can see that x needs to be between the values of 3/8 and 1/2 since 3 ÷ 8 = 3/8 and 4 ÷ 8 = 4/8 = 1/2. Now compare these to the other fractions. 2/3 and 3/5 are greater than 1/2, while 1/8 is less than 3/8.

Therefore, the correct answer must be 2/5. To check this, insert the fractions from the answer choices for the value of x. Then complete the multiplication and division to see which fraction meets the criteria stated in the problem.

$3 < 8x < 4$

$3 < 8 \times {}^2/_5 < 4$

$3 < [(8 \times 2) \div 5] < 4$

$3 < (16 \div 5) < 4$

$3 < 3.2 < 4$

37) The correct answer is C.
Step 1 – Take the total number of employees and divide this by 5.
$250 \div 5 = 50$
Step 2 – The question asks how many questionnaires have not been completed and returned, so subtract to find the amount in the 'not returned' subset.
$5 - 4 = 1$
Step 3 – Multiply the result from step 2 by the result from step 1 to solve.
$50 \times 1 = 50$

38) The correct answer is D. Take the total dollar amount and multiply by the 27% for schools:
$\$5,275,300 \times 0.27 = \$1,424,331$

39) The correct answer is B.
First, find the intersection of P and Q.
Look at sets P and Q and highlight the numbers that they have in common:
P = {**3**, 6, **9**, 12, 15} Q = {1, **3**, 5, 7, **9**, 11}
So P ∩ Q = {3, 9}.
Set R before its intersection with the intersection of P and Q was {0, 1, 9, 81}
So, highlight the numbers that the previous result has in common with set R:
P ∩ Q = {3, **9**} R = {0, 1, **9**, 81}
So, the answer is {9}.

40) The correct answer is A.
Factor out xy: $15xy - 20x^2y - 40y^2x^2 = xy(15 - 20x - 40xy)$
Then, factor out the common factor of 5:
$xy(15 - 20x - 40xy) = 5xy(3 - 4x - 8xy)$

41) The correct answer is A.
Step 1 – Calculate how many minutes there are in 40 hours.
40 hours × 60 minutes per hour = 2400 minutes
Step 2 – Divide the number of prescriptions into the previous result to get the rate.
$2400 \div 250 = 9.6$ minutes per prescription

42) The correct answer is B.
The formula for the area of a triangle is: ${}^1/_2 \times$ base × height
The triangle has a height of 4 inches and a base of 3 inches, so put the values into the formula to solve:
${}^1/_2 \times$ base × height =
${}^1/_2 \times 3 \times 4 =$
${}^1/_2 \times 12 = 6$

43) The correct answer is D. Our data set is: 5, 4, 6, 11, 12, 14, 15, 7, 8, 10, 13, 9
Mode is a measure of frequency, so the value that occurs most frequently in the data set is the mode. No number in the set occurs more than once. So, there is no mode.

44) The correct answer is A. Add the distance from Bellevue to Poplar Falls to the distance from Poplar Falls and Wayward Pines to find the total distance in meters: 1,500 + 1,200 = 2,700. Convert meters to millimeters by multiplying by 1,000 since 1 meter = 1,000 millimeters: 2,700 meters × 1,000 = 2,700,000 millimeters

45) The correct answer is D. Any number to the power of zero is equal to 1. So, substitute 1 for b^0 to solve: $a \times b^0 = a \times 1 = a$

46) The correct answer is A.
Substitute the values provided in the answer choices into the equation to solve:
$y = 2x + 5$
$y = (2 \times 1) + 5$
$y = 2 + 5$
$y = 7$
So, (1, 7) is the correct answer.

47) The correct answer is C. The formula for the volume of a cylinder is $\pi \times R^2 \times$ height. Since the base of the cylinder forms a circle, $\pi \times R^2$ is equal to the area of the base of the cylinder. So, put the values into the formula to solve:
$640\pi = \pi \times R^2 \times$ height
$640\pi = \pi \times R^2 \times 10$
$640\pi \div 10 = \pi \times R^2 \times 10 \div 10$
$64\pi = \pi \times R^2$

48) The correct answer is D. There are no parentheses or exponents, so do the multiplication and division from left to right.
$12 + 15 - 300 \div 100 \times 3 - 180 + 9 =$
$12 + 15 - (300 \div 100) \times 3 - 180 + 9 =$
$12 + 15 - 3 \times 3 - 180 + 9 =$
$12 + 15 - (3 \times 3) - 180 + 9 =$
$12 + 15 - 9 - 180 + 9$
Then do the addition and subtraction from left to right.
$12 + 15 - 9 - 180 + 9 =$
$27 - 9 - 180 + 9 =$
$18 - 180 + 9 =$
$-162 + 9 = -153$

49) The correct answer is C.
Multiply the integers in front of the variables, and add the exponents.
$(5ab^5)(-6ab^3) =$
$(5 \times -6)(a \times a)(b^{5+3}) =$
$-30a^2b^8$

50) The correct answer is C. The dentist has seen twenty patients. The median is the value that is in the middle of a data set when the values have been placed in ascending order.
If the data set has an even number of items, we have to take the average of the two middle

values to calculate the median. Put the data in ascending order first:
0, 0, 0, 1, 1, 1, 2, 2, 2, **2, 2**, 3, 3, 3, 3, 4, 4, 5, 6, 7
We have two values in the middle, so we need to take the average of these to find the median:
(2 + 2) ÷ 2 = 2
So, the median is 2.

1) A store sells domestic cleaning products. A certain type of liquid cleaner is sold in increments of 1/4 of a cup. Each 1/4 of a cup costs 50 cents. One customer buys $10^1/_4$ cups of this cleaner. How much will she pay for this purchase?
   A) $5.13
   B) $5.50
   C) $10.50
   D) $20.50

2) The cost of sales figures each month for a company's first five months of business this year were: $723, $618, $576, $812, and $984. What was the total cost of sales for the first five months of business this year?
   A) $743
   B) $3,623
   C) $3,713
   D) $3,722

3) 4 out of every 5 employee-satisfaction questionnaires have been completed and returned. If a company has 250 total employees, and every employee must complete and return the questionnaire, how many questionnaires have not been completed and returned?
   A) 4
   B) 5
   C) 50
   D) 200

4) A flower store sells poinsettia plants for $20 during December and for $12 during January. In December, 55 customers purchased poinsettias, and 20 customers purchased them in January. How much money did the store receive for poinsettia sales during December and January?
   A) $240
   B) $1,060
   C) $1,100
   D) $1,340

5) During each flight, a flight attendant is required to count the number of passengers on board the aircraft. The morning flight had 52 passengers more than the evening flight, and there were 540 passengers in total on the two flights that day. How many passengers were there on the evening flight?
   A) 244
   B) 296
   C) 488
   D) 540

6) A cafeteria serves spaghetti to senior citizens on Fridays. The spaghetti comes prepared in large containers, and each container holds 15 servings of spaghetti. The cafeteria is expecting 82 senior citizens this Friday. What is the least number of containers of spaghetti that the cafeteria will need in order to serve all 82 people?
A) 4
B) 5
C) 6
D) 7

7) A worm can crawl 10.5 inches in 45 seconds. How far will it crawl in 6 minutes?
A) 45 inches
B) 63 inches
C) 64 inches
D) 84 inches

8) Each week, a company tabulates the results of customer satisfaction surveys by region and calculates the bonuses to be paid. The company has four regions, each of which has one salesperson. Salespeople in each region receive bonuses based on the amount of positive customer feedback they receive. The results of the surveys were as follows:
Region 1: 40 positive customer feedback results
Region 2: 30 positive customer feedback results
Region 3: 20 positive customer feedback results
Region 4: 30 positive customer feedback results
If the four salespeople received $540 in bonuses in total, how much bonus money does the company pay each individual salesperson per satisfied customer?
A) $4.00
B) $4.50
C) $4.90
D) $5.00

9) Return on investment (ROI) percentages for seven companies were: –2%, 5%, 7.5%, 14%, 17%, 1.3%, –3%. Which figure below best approximates the mean ROI for the seven companies?
A) 2%
B) 5.7%
C) 6.25%
D) 7.5%

10) The students in an English Language Academy have been asked about their plans to attend a weekend language workshop. The chart below shows the responses by class percentages. Which figure below best approximates the percentage of the total number of students from all four classes that will attend the workshop? Note that each class has 30 students.

	Will Attend	Will Not Attend	Undecided
Class A:	45%	24%	31%
Class B:	30%	45%	25%
Class C:	38%	20%	42%
Class D:	30%	25%	45%

A) 25%
B) 35%

C) 45%
D) 55%

11) An employment agency for temporary employees charges clients $15 per hour for each hour the temporary employee works. The agency pays each temporary employee $12 an hour and retains the difference as a commission. The agency had 10 employees who worked 40 hours each this week. How much did the agency make on commission for these 10 employees this week?
A) $30.00
B) $120.00
C) $1,200.00
D) $4,800.00

12) 49 out of the 50 items in a company's product line had above average sales this month. What percentage of the items in the product line had above average sales this month?
A) 0.098%
B) 0.98%
C) 9.80%
D) 98%

13) Sales each day for the past five days have been as follows: $90, $85, $85, $105, $110. What was the daily average sales amount during this five-day period?
A) $25
B) $85
C) $90
D) $95

14) A fabric store sells ribbon in 3-inch or one-foot increments. One customer wanted two types of ribbon, and she bought $8^3/_4$ feet of one type of ribbon and $7^1/_2$ feet of another type. How much ribbon did this customer buy in total?
A) 7 feet and 6 inches
B) 8 feet and 9 inches
C) 15 feet and 3 inches
D) 16 feet and 3 inches

15) Hours spent on a work order are recorded by the tenth of an hour in 6 minute increments. For a particular work order, $28^3/_{10}$ hours in total have been budgeted. $7^9/_{10}$ hours have already been spent on the work order. Which amount below represents the amount of time left for this work order?
A) $36^1/_5$
B) $35^6/_{10}$
C) $20^2/_5$
D) $20^3/_5$

16) A decorative stone mix requires 2 parts of white gravel for every 3 parts of blue slate chippings. An order requires 147 parts of blue slate chippings. How many parts of white gravel should be added?
A) 73.5
B) 88.0

C) 98.0
D) 220.5

17) A factory manufactures absorbent disposable products that consist of a single layer of absorbent cotton wadding on the inside and a double layer polyvinyl carbonate sheeting on the outside. Each layer of absorbent cotton wadding is 18 inches long, and each layer of polyvinyl carbonate sheeting is 19 inches long. 18 of these products need to be made for a single order. How many feet of materials in total will be required to manufacture this order?
A) 55.5
B) 56
C) 84
D) 666

18) An automotive store can buy a case containing 24 bottles of motor oil for $50 a case wholesale. Individual bottles of this brand of motor oil cost $2.50 per bottle wholesale. What is the best price the store will pay if it buys 100 bottles of motor oil wholesale?
A) $200.00
B) $200.10
C) $202.50
D) $210.00

19) Flavored rice cakes sold in the United States are measured in ounces, and units sold overseas are measured in grams. 39 ounces of flavoring are needed for a batch of rice cakes for the United States and 1,190.7 grams of the same flavoring are needed for another batch of rice cakes to be sold overseas. How much flavoring is needed for both batches in total?
A) 81 ounces
B) 40.48 ounces
C) 43.38 grams
D) 2,297.35 grams

20) A ceiling is 25 feet wide and 35 feet long. The ceiling is to be covered with square ceiling tiles that measure 6 inches by 6 inches each. How many of these square ceiling tiles are needed to install this ceiling?
A) 1,750
B) 3,500
C) 480
D) 875

21) This month, a nurse dispensed 1,275,000 milligrams of medication to patients. How many grams of medication were dispensed?
A) 127.5
B) 1,275
C) 12,750
D) 127,500,000

22) A basketball has a diameter of 10 inches. Which figure below best represents the volumetric capacity of the basketball in cubic centimeters?
A) 32
B) 523
C) 4,824
D) 8,576

23) Cell phone covers are sold for a retail price of $12 per unit. This amounts to a 525% markup over the cost for each unit. How much does each unit cost?
A) $0.192
B) $1.92
C) $6.25
D) $0.75

24) The perimeter of a rectangle is 350 feet and the width of the shortest side is 75 feet. What is the measurement of the length of the rectangle?
A) 10 feet
B) 90 feet
C) 95 feet
D) 100 feet

25) Storage boxes for rice flour measure 3 feet by 3 feet by 2 feet each. The first box is $^{1}/_{6}$ full, the second box is $^{1}/_{2}$ full, and the third box is $^{2}/_{3}$ full. A factory wants to replenish its supply of rice flour so that it will have three full boxes. The rice flour costs 9 cents a cubic inch. To the nearest dollar, what will it cost to replenish the stock in the three boxes?
A) $270
B) $466
C) $998
D) $4,666

26) An entertainer pulls colored ribbons out of a box at random for a dance routine. The box contains 5 red ribbons and 6 blue ribbons. The other ribbons in the box are green. If a ribbon is pulled out of the box at random, the probability that the ribbon is red is $^{1}/_{3}$. How many green ribbons are in the box?
A) 3
B) 4
C) 5
D) 6

27) Find the median of the following: 2.5, 9.4, 3.1, 1.7, 3.2, 8.2, 4.5, 6.4, 7.8
A) 3.2
B) 4.5
C) 5.2
D) 6.4

28) For the functions $f_2(x)$ below, x and y are positive integers greater than 10. If $f_1(x) = x^2$, which of the functions below has the greatest value for $f_1(f_2(x))$?
A) $f_2(x) = x + y$
B) $f_2(x) = (xy)^2$
C) $f_2(x) = xy$
D) $f_2(x) = x - y$

29) In the xy plane, line B passes through the origin and is parallel to line A. Line A passes through the points (0, 4) and (2, 12). The slope of line B could be which one of the following?
A) 4
B) –4
C) $^1/_4$
D) $-^1/_4$

30) The rectangular solid below has a length of 14 inches a height of 6 inches and a depth of 5 inches. What is the surface area of the rectangular solid in square inches?

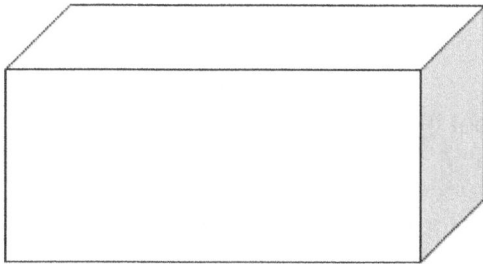

A) 200
B) 336
C) 368
D) 396

31) Which expression is equivalent to the following? $^x/_8 + ^y/_3$
A) $^{x + y}/_{11}$
B) $^{3x + 8y}/_{24}$
C) $^{8x + 3y}/_{24}$
D) $^{3x + 8y}/_{11}$

32) The cost of tacos, with T being the total cost in dollars and N being the number of tacos, is represented by the equation $T = ^{17}/_2 \times N$. The cost of a soft drink is represented by the equation $C = ^9/_4 \times D$, with C being the total cost in dollars and D being the number of soft drinks. What is the cost for one taco and one soft drink?
A) $2.25
B) $6.25
C) $8.50
D) $10.75

33) The graph below most closely approximates which of the following functions?

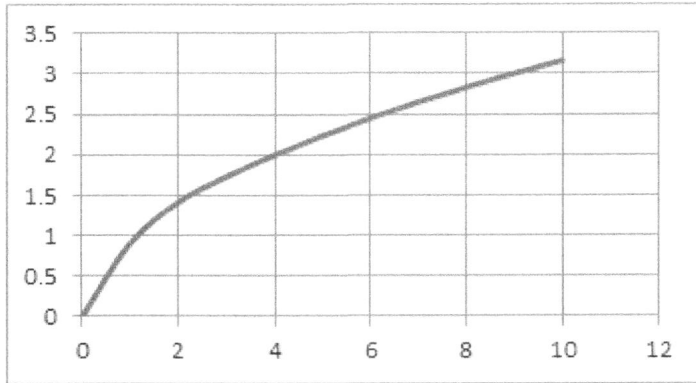

A) $f(x) = x^2 + x$

B) $f(x) = \frac{1}{x}$

C) $f(x) = \sqrt{x}$

D) $f(x) = 2^x$

34) Which of the following is equivalent to the expression $3(x + 5)(x - 2)$ for all values of x?
   A) $3x^2 + 9x - 30$
   B) $3x^2 + 3x - 10$
   C) $3x^2 - 9x - 30$
   D) $3x^2 + 9x + 30$

35) If $5x + 9 > x + 25$, then x could be which of the following?
   A) $^{12}/_3$
   B) $^{18}/_5$
   C) $^{21}/_4$
   D) $^{15}/_4$

36) What is the value of $f_1(4)$ where $f_1(x) = 3^x$?
   A)   64
   B)   12
   C)   81
   D) 4^4

37) Which of the following best describes the range of $y = x^2 - 52$?
   A)   All real numbers.
   B) $y \geq 0$
   C) $y \leq -52$
   D) $y \geq -52$

38) What are two possible values of x for the following equation? $x^2 + 5x + 6 = 0$
   A)   −2 and −3
   B)   −5 and −6
   C)   5 and 6
   D)   2 and 3

39) If $f(x) = x \div (3 + x)$ and $g(x) = 1 \div (x - 2)$, what is the domain of the function $f + g$?
   A) $\{-3, 0\}$
   B) All real numbers.
   C) All real numbers except 0.
   D) All real numbers except -3 and 2.

40) What is an equivalent for the following? $\sqrt{192}$
   A) $1 \div 50$
   B) $3\sqrt{8}$
   C) $8\sqrt{3}$
   D) $64\sqrt{3}$

41) Perform the operation: $(2ab - 3a)(5ab^3 - 2b^2 + 4a)$
   A) $10a^2b^4 - 4ab^3 + 8ab - 15a^2b^3 + 6ab^2 - 12a^2$
   B) $10a^2b^4 - 4ab^3 + 8a^2b - 15a^2b^3 + 6ab^2 - 12a^2$
   C) $10a^2b^4 - 4ab^3 + 8a^2b - 15a^2b^3 + 6ab^2 + 12a^2$
   D) $10a^2b^4 - 4ab^3 + 8a^2b - 15b^3 + 6ab^2 - 12a^2$

42) The central angle in a circle is 36° and is subtended by an arc which is 16π centimeters in length. How long is the radius of this circle?
   A)   160 centimeters
   B)   80 centimeters
   C)   80π centimeters
   D)   10 centimeters

43) In the function $f(x) = a(x^2)(x + 5)$, a is an integer constant. The end behavior of the graph of $y = f(x)$ is negative for large positive values of x and positive for large negative values of x. Which of the following statements is true with respect to the leading coefficient?
   A) The leading coefficient is negative.
   B) The leading coefficient is positive.
   C) The leading coefficient is an odd number.
   D) The leading coefficient is an even number.

44) Express the following as a logarithmic function and solve for x: $2^{3x} = 64$
   A) $3x = \log_2 64$; $x = 6$
   B) $3x = \log_2 64$; $x = 2$
   C) $2 = \log_{3x} 64$; $x = 6$
   D) $2 = \log_{3x} 64$; $x = 2$

45) Simplify then factor: $(x + 1)(x - 2) + (x + 1)^2 - x(x + 1)$
   A) $2x^2 - x^2 + x - 1$
   B) $2x^2 - x^2 - x - 1$
   C) $(x + 1)(x + 1)$
   D) $(x + 1)(x - 1)$

46) Find the equivalent for the following expression:

$$\frac{x^2}{x^2 + x} + \frac{5}{x} = ?$$

A) $\dfrac{x + 5x + 5}{x^2 + 2x}$

B) $\dfrac{x^2 + 5}{x^2 + x}$

C) $\dfrac{5 + 10x}{x^3}$

D) $\dfrac{x^2 + 5x + 5}{x^2 + x}$

47) Triangle ABC and triangle XYZ are shown in the illustration below. ∠A is congruent to ∠X. Which of the following must also be true for triangles ABC and XYZ to be congruent? (Note that the drawing is not necessarily drawn to scale.)

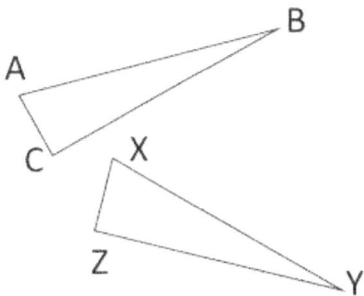

A) ∠B = ∠Y
B) ∠C = ∠Z
C) ∠C = ∠Z and side AC = side XZ
D) ∠C = ∠Z and ∠B = ∠Y

48) A kite is formed of two identical isosceles triangles that are joined together by their bases in the center of the kite. Each isosceles triangle has a base of 2 feet and a height of 3 feet. What is the perimeter measurement of the kite?
   A) 6
   B) 12
   C) $2\sqrt{10}$
   D) $4\sqrt{10}$

49) Which of the following could be an equation of the graph below?

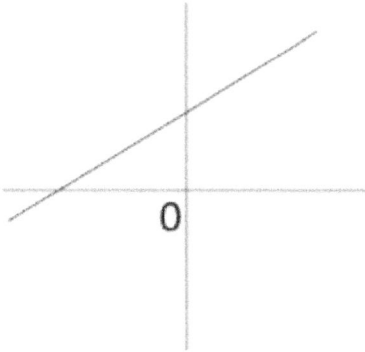

A) $y = x^2 + 3$
B) $y = x + 5$
C) $y = -x + 7$
D) $y = |x| - 5$

50) $x^{\frac{3}{8}} = ?$

A) $\left(\sqrt[8]{x}\right)^3$

B) $\left(\sqrt[3]{x}\right)^8$

C) $\left(3\sqrt{x}\right)^8$

D) 8

Answers and Explanations for CHSPE Math Practice Test 6

1) The correct answer is D. Convert the cups to quarter cups: 10 cups = 40 quarter cups. Then combine the whole number with the fraction and multiply to solve: $40\frac{1}{4}$ × 50 cents per quarter cup = 40.25 × 0.50 = $20.50

2) The correct answer is C. The problem is asking for the total for all five months, so we add the amounts together to solve: $723 + $618 + $576 + $812 + $984 = $3,713

3) The correct answer is C. Step 1 – Take the total number of employees and divide this by 5: 250 ÷ 5 = 50. Step 2 – The question asks how many questionnaires have not been completed and returned, so subtract to find the amount in the 'not returned' subset: 5 – 4 = 1. Step 3 – Multiply the result from step 2 by the result from step 1 to solve: 50 × 1 = 50

4) The correct answer is D. Step 1 – Determine the total for sales in December: $20 × 55 = $1,100. Step 2 – Determine the total sales for January: $12 × 20 = $240. Step 3 – Add these two amounts to solve: $1,100 + $240 = $1,340

5) The correct answer is A. The problem tells us that the morning flight had 52 passengers more than the evening flight, and there were 540 passengers in total on the two flights that day. Step 1 – First of all, we need to deduct the difference from the total: 540 – 52 = 488. In other words, there were 488 passengers on both flights combined, plus the 52 additional passengers on the morning flight. Step 2 – Now divide this result by 2 to allocate a number of passengers to each flight: 488 ÷ 2 = 244 passengers on the evening flight. (Had the question asked you for the number of passengers on the morning flight, you would have had to add back the number of additional passengers to find the total amount of passengers for the morning flight: 244 + 52 = 296 passengers on the morning flight)

6) The correct answer is C. Divide and then round up: 82 people in total ÷ 15 people served per container = 5.467 containers. We need to round up to 6 since we cannot purchase a fractional part of a container.

7) The correct answer is D. The question is asking us about a time duration of 6 minutes, so we need to calculate the number of seconds in 6 minutes: 6 minutes × 60 seconds per minute = 360 seconds in total. Then divide the total time by the amount of time needed to make one journey: 360 seconds ÷ 45 seconds per journey = 8 journeys. Finally, multiply the number of journeys by the number of inches per journey in order to get the total inches: 10.5 inches for 1 journey × 8 journeys = 84 inches in total

8) The correct answer is B. First of all, add up to find the total number of customers: 40 + 30 + 20 + 30 = 120 customers in total for all four regions. The salespeople received $540 in total, so we need to divide this by the number of customers: $540 ÷ 120 customers = $4.50 per customer

9) The correct answer is B. The mean is the arithmetic average. First, find the total for all seven companies: –2% + 5% + 7.5% + 14% + 17% + 1.3% + –3% = 39.8%. Then divide by 7 since there are 7 companies in the set: 39.8% ÷ 7 = 5.68% ≈ 5.7%

10) The correct answer is B. 45% of class A, 30% of class B, 38% of class C, and 30% of class D will attend. Since each of the four classes has the same number of students, we can simply divide by 4 to get the average. Calculating the average, we get the overall

95

percentage for all four glasses: (45 + 30 + 38 + 30) ÷ 4 = 35.75%. 35% is the closest answer to 35.75%, so it best approximates our result.

11) The correct answer is C. Step 1 – Determine the commission earned per hour: $15 charged – $12 paid to employee = $3 per hour commission. Step 2 – Calculate the total hours that the 10 employees worked: 10 × 40 = 400 hours in total. Step 3 – Multiply the total number of hours by the commission per hour to solve: 400 hours × $3 commission per hour = $1,200 total commission

12) The correct answer is D. Divide to solve: 49 ÷ 50 = 0.98 = 98%

13) The correct answer is D. Calculate the total, and divide by the number of days. Step 1 – Find the total: $90 + $85 + $85 + $105 + $110 = $475. Step 2 – Divide the result from Step 1 by the number of days: $475 ÷ 5 = $95

14) The correct answer is D. Step 1 – Add the whole numbers: 8 + 7 = 15. Step 2 – Add the fractions: 3/4 + 1/2 = 3/4 + 2/4 = 5/4. Step 3 – Simplify the fraction from Step 2: 5/4 = 4/4 + 1/4 = $1\frac{1}{4}$ = 1 foot and 3 inches. Step 4 – Combine the results from Step 1 and Step 3 to solve the problem: 15 feet + 1 foot and 3 inches = 16 feet and 3 inches

15) The correct answer is C. In this problem, the fraction on the second number is larger than the fraction on the first number, so we need to convert the first fraction before we start our calculation. Step 1 – Convert $28\frac{3}{10}$ for subtraction: $28\frac{3}{10}$ = $27\frac{3}{10}$ + 1 = $27\frac{3}{10}$ + $\frac{10}{10}$ = $27\frac{13}{10}$. Step 2 – Subtract the whole numbers. $7\frac{9}{10}$ hours have been spent on the job so far, so subtract the 7 hours: 27 – 7 = 20. Step 3 – Subtract the fractions: 13/10 – 9/10 = 4/10. Step 4 – Simplify the fraction from Step 3: 4/10 =   (4 ÷ 2)/(10 ÷ 2) = 2/5. Step 4 – Combine the results from Step 2 and Step 4 to get your new mixed number to solve the problem: 20 + 2/5 = $20\frac{2}{5}$

16) The correct answer is C. Step 1 – Take the 147 parts of blue slate chippings for this order and divide by the 3 parts stated in the original ratio: 147 ÷ 3 = 49. Step 2 – Multiply the result from Step 1 by the 2 parts of white gravel stated in the original ratio to get your answer: 49 × 2 = 98

17) The correct answer is C. Step 1 – Determine the total amount of inches of material needed for one unit. Don't forget that the second material needs to be doubled because there is a double layer of this material: 18 + 19 + 19 = 56 inches. Step 2 – Calculate how many inches are needed in total: 56 inches per unit × 18 units = 1008 inches in total. Step 3 – Convert the inches to feet: 1008 inches ÷ 12 = 84 feet

18) The correct answer is D. Step 1 – Determine the excess amount over the amount for the deal: 100 bottles needed – (4 cases × 24 bottles each) = 100 – 96 = 4 individual bottles left. Step 2 – Take the result from the previous step and multiply by the individual price: 4 × $2.50 = $10. Step 3 – Determine the cost of the 4 cases: 4 × $50 = $200. Step 4 – Add the results from the previous two steps to get the total wholesale price for the deal: $200 + $10 = $210

19) The correct answer is A. Step 1 – Convert the grams to ounces: 1190.7 ÷ 28.35 = 42. Step 2 – Add the result from step 1 to the number of ounces for the US order to solve: 39 + 42 = 81 ounces

20) The correct answer is B. Step 1 – Find the area of the ceiling. The formula for the area of a rectangle is (length × width). So, substitute the values to find the area: (35 × 25) = 875 square feet. Step 2 – Find the area of each ceiling tile. The measurements for our tiles are given in inches: 6 inches by 6 inches = 36 square inches. Step 3 – Calculate how many square inches there are in a square foot: 12 inches by 12 inches = 144 square inches. Step 4 – Determine how many tiles you need per square foot: 144 square inches ÷ 36 square inches per tile = 4 tiles per square foot. Step 5 – Multiply to solve: 875 square feet in total × 4 tiles per square foot = 3,500 tiles needed

21) The correct answer is B. From the formula sheet, we can see that 1 milligram = 0.001 gram. We are converting milligrams to grams, so we are doing the formula in the correct order, rather than in reverse. Therefore, multiply by 0.001 to solve: 1,275,000 milligrams × 0.001 = 1,275 grams

22) The correct answer is D. Step 1 – Find the radius in centimeters. The diameter is 10 inches, so the radius is 5 inches. 1 inch = 2.54 centimeters, so multiply to determine the length of the radius in centimeters: 5 × 2.54 = 12.7 centimeters. Step 2 – Cube the radius for the formula: 12.7 × 12.7 × 12.7 = 2048.38. Then multiply by 3.14 and 4/3 to find the volume of the sphere: 2048.38 × 3.14 × 4/3 = 8575.8968, which we round up to 8,576.

23) The correct answer is B. To calculate a reverse percentage you need to divide, rather than multiply. So, take the $12 retail price and divide by 625%, which is 100% for the cost plus 525% for the markup: $12 ÷ 625% = $12 ÷ 6.25 = $1.92

24) The correct answer is D. The perimeter of rectangle is 2(*length* + *width*). So, determine the total width for both sides: 2 × 75 = 150. Now deduct this amount from the perimeter: 350 – 150 = 200. Finally, divide this result by 2 to get the length: 200 ÷ 2 = 100

25) The correct answer is D. Step 1 – Calculate the cubic inches for each box: length × width × height = 3 × 3 × 2 = 18 cubic feet per box × 1,728 cubic inches per cubic foot = 31,104 cubic inches per box. Step 2 – Determine how much of the product is on hand. The first box is $1/6$ full, the second box is $1/2$ full, and the third box is $2/3$ full: $1/6$ + $1/2$ + $2/3$ = $1/6$ + $3/6$ + $4/6$ = $8/6$.= $1^2/6$ = $1^1/3$ boxes left. Step 3 – Determine how much is required to replenish the stock: 3 boxes needed – $1^1/3$ boxes on hand = $1^2/3$ boxes needed. Step 4 – Determine how many cubic inches are needed: $1^2/3$ boxes needed × 31,104 cubic inches per box = 51,840 cubic inches needed. Step 5 – Calculate the cost of the cubic inches: 51,840 cubic inches needed × 0.09 per cubic inch = $4,665.60, which we round to $4,666.

26) The correct answer is B. This question is asking you to determine the value missing from a sample space when calculating basic probability. This is like other problems on basic probability, but we need to work backwards to find the missing value. First, set up an equation to find the total items in the sample space. Then subtract the quantities of the known subsets from the total in order to determine the missing value. We will use variable *T* as the total number of items in the set. The probability of getting a red ribbon is $1/3$.

So, set up an equation to find the total items in the data set:

$$\frac{5}{T} = \frac{1}{3}$$

$$\frac{5}{T} \times 3 = \frac{1}{3} \times 3$$

$$\frac{5}{T} \times 3 = 1$$

$$\frac{15}{T} = 1$$

$$\frac{15}{T} \times T = 1 \times T$$

$$15 = T$$

We have 5 red ribbons, 6 blue ribbons, and x green ribbons in the data set that make up the total sample space, so now subtract the amount of red and blue ribbons from the total in order to determine the number of green ribbons.
$5 + 6 + x = 15$
$11 + x = 15$
$11 - 11 + x = 15 - 11$
$x = 4$

27) The correct answer is B. Our data set is: 2.5, 9.4, 3.1, 1.7, 3.2, 8.2, 4.5, 6.4, 7.8. First, put the numbers in ascending order: 1.7, 2.5, 3.1, 3.2, 4.5, 6.4, 7.8, 8.2, 9.4. The median is the number in the middle of the set: 1.7, 2.5, 3.1, 3.2, **4.5**, 6.4, 7.8, 8.2, 9.4

28) The correct answer is B. $f_2(x)$ is the function in the inner parentheses, so the value calculated for $f_2(x)$ will be used for the variable x in the function $f_1(x)$. $(xy)^2$ will always be greater than xy, x − y or x + y for the conditions stated in the facts of this problem. Accordingly, the result will be greatest when xy is squared. If you are unsure, insert values for x and y to test the result.

29) The correct answer is A. In this question, we first need to calculate the slope of line A. Using the slope formula, we can calculate the slope of line A as follows: $[y_2 - y_1]/[x_2 - x_1]$
Put in the values for x and y from the two pairs of coordinates in the problem:
$[y_2 - y_1]/[x_2 - x_1] =$
$[12 - 4]/[2 - 0] =$
$^8/_2 = 4$
Parallel lines are equal in slope, so the slope of the parallel line will also have a slope of 4.

30) The correct answer is C. The surface area of a rectangular solid is found by finding the sum of the areas of each face of the solid. Calculate the area of the each of the 2 rectangular panels for the front and back of the box: 14 × 6 = 84. There are two of these panels, so the total surface area for these is: 84 × 2 = 168. Calculate the area of the each of the 2 rectangular panels for the top and bottom of the box: 14 × 5 = 70. There are two of these panels, so the total surface area for these is: 70 × 4 = 140. Then calculate the surface area for the two end panels. Each end panel is 6 by 5: 6 × 5 = 30. There are two of these, so multiply by two to get the total for this part of the solid. 30 × 2 = 60. Then add the three amounts together to solve. 168 + 140 + 60 = 368

31) The correct answer is B. Find the lowest common denominator. Then add the numerators together as shown:

$x/8 + y/3 =$

$[x/8 \times 3/3] + [y/3 \times 8/8] =$

$3x/24 + 8y/24 = 3x + 8y/24$

32) The correct answer is D. This question asks you to interpret equations in order to determine the unit prices of two items. The fractions in each equation represent the per unit cost.

So, find the price of one taco: $17/2 = 17 \div 2 = \$8.50$

Then find the cost for one soft drink: $9/4 = 9 \div 4 = \$2.25$

Then add these two results together to get the total to solve: $\$8.50 + \$2.25 = \$10.75$

33) The correct answer is C. First of all, make some general observations about the data. There is a direct relationship between x and y, so as x increases, y also increases. Also note that there are no negative values. Then look at specific points to help you choose the correct function. We can see that for y = 2, x = 4. Since 2 is the square root of 4, we know that we need to choose answer C. This also fits because there is no real number solution for the square root of a negative number.

34) The correct answer is A. You should use the FOIL (first, inside, outside, last) method in this problem. Be very careful with the negative numbers when doing the multiplication.

$3(x + 5)(x - 2) =$

$3[(x \times x) + (x \times -2) + (5 \times x) + (5 \times -2)] =$

$3(x^2 + -2x + 5x + -10) =$

$3(x^2 - 2x + 5x - 10) =$

$3(x^2 + 3x - 10) =$

$3x^2 + 9x - 30$

35) The correct answer is C. Perform operations on each side of the inequality to isolate x:

$5x + 9 > x + 25$

$5x + 9 - 9 > x + 25 - 9$

$5x > x + 16$

$5x - x > x - x + 16$

$4x > 16$

$x > 16 \div 4$

$x > 16/4$

$x > 4$

$21/4 = 5.25$, which is the only answer greater than 4, so C is the correct answer.

36) The correct answer is C. Put the value provided for x into the function to solve.

$f_1(x) = 3^x$

$f_1(4) = 3^x$

$3^4 = 81$

37) The correct answer is D. The range of a function is all possible y values or "outputs" for the function. $x^2 - 52$ will yield a result of –52 when x = 0. $x^2 - 52$ will result in a number greater than –52 for all other positive or negative values of x. Therefore, the range will always be equal to or greater than –52.

38) The correct answer is A.
Step 1: Factor the equation.
First of all, look at the third term of the equation, which is 6. So, find the factors of 6:
$1 \times 6 = 6$ and $2 \times 3 = 6$.
The second term of the equation contains a 5, so we need two factors that add up to five.
Choose 2 and 3 since $2 + 3 = 5$.
Then factor the equation like this:
$x^2 + 5x + 6 = 0$
$(x + 2)(x + 3) = 0$
Step 2: Now substitute 0 for x in the first pair of parentheses.
$(0 + 2)(x + 3) = 0$
$2(x + 3) = 0$
$2x + 6 = 0$
$2x + 6 - 6 = 0 - 6$
$2x = -6$
$2x \div 2 = -6 \div 2$
$x = -3$
Step 3: Then substitute 0 for x in the second pair of parentheses.
$(x + 2)(x + 3) = 0$
$(x + 2)(0 + 3) = 0$
$(x + 2)3 = 0$
$3x + 6 = 0$
$3x + 6 - 6 = 0 - 6$
$3x = -6$
$3x \div 3 = -6 \div 3$
$x = -2$

39) The correct answer is D. Remember that the domain of a function is all possible x values for the function. You need to avoid any mathematical operations that do not have real number solutions, such as dividing by a zero or finding the square root of a negative number. $f(x) = x \div (3 + x)$, so to avoid dividing by a zero, $x \neq -3$. $g(x) = 1 \div (x - 2)$, so $x \neq 2$. To find the domain of both functions, put these two results together to state the exclusions to the domain. Therefore, the domain of $f + g$ is all real numbers except -3 and 2.

40) The correct answer is C. To simplify radicals, you first need to find the factors for the number inside the radical sign.
The factors of 192 are as follows: $1 \times 192 = 192$; $2 \times 96 = 192$; $3 \times 64 = 192$; $4 \times 48 = 192$; $6 \times 32 = 192$; $8 \times 24 = 192$; $12 \times 16 = 192$.
If any of your factors are perfect squares, you can simplify the radical.
64 is the greatest factor that is a perfect square, so you need to factor inside the radical sign as shown to solve the problem:
$\sqrt{192} = \sqrt{64 \times 3} =$
$\sqrt{8^2 \times 3} = \sqrt{8^2} \times \sqrt{3} =$
$8 \times \sqrt{3} = 8\sqrt{3}$

41) The correct answer is B.
Step 1: Apply the distributive property of multiplication by multiplying the first term in the first set of parentheses by all of the terms inside the second pair of parentheses. Then multiply the second term from the first set of parentheses by all of the terms inside the second set of parentheses.

100

Expand the expression:
$(2ab - 3a)(5ab^3 - 2b^2 + 4a) =$
$(2ab \times 5ab^3) + (2ab \times -2b^2) + (2ab \times 4a) + (-3a \times 5ab^3) + (-3a \times -2b^2) + (-3a \times 4a)$
Step 2: Multiply and add up the individual products in order to solve the problem:
$(2ab \times 5ab^3) + (2ab \times -2b^2) + (2ab \times 4a) + (-3a \times 5ab^3) + (-3a \times -2b^2) + (-3a \times 4a) =$
$10a^2b^4 - 4ab^3 + 8a^2b - 15a^2b^3 + 6ab^2 - 12a^2$

42) The correct answer is B. The angle given in the problem is 36°. If we divide the total of 360° in the circle by the 36° angle, we have: $360 \div 36 = 10$. You can think of arc length as the partial circumference of a circle, so we can visualize that there are 10 such arcs along this circle. We can then multiply the number of arcs by the length of each arc to get the circumference of the circle:
$10 \times 16\pi = 160\pi$ (circumference)
Finally, use the formula for the circumference of the circle to solve.
Circumference = $\pi \times$ radius $\times 2$
$160\pi = \pi \times 2 \times$ radius
$160\pi \div 2 = \pi \times 2 \times$ radius $\div 2$
$80\pi = \pi \times$ radius
$80 =$ radius

43) The correct answer is A. The end behavior of a graph refers to the values of the polynomial function as it approaches positive or negative infinity. The coefficient that is first in a polynomial as is called a leading coefficient. So, the leading coefficient in this question is variable a. When the parentheticals are multiplied together, the result will be positive when x is a large positive number. The result will be negative when x is a large negative number. If the output is negative for large positive values of x, then a must be negative. This is because the result of the multiplication of the parentheticals will be positive when x is positive, and we would then need to multiply by a negative number to get a negative output. If the output is positive for large negative values of x, then a must again be negative. This is because the result of the multiplication of the parentheticals will be negative when x is negative, and we would then need to multiply by another negative number to get a positive output.

44) The correct answer is B.
$2^{3x} = 64$ is the same as $3x = \log_2 64$.
If $2^{3x} = 64$, we need to multiply 2 times itself to get the correct value.
$2 \times 2 \times 2 \times 2 \times 2 \times 2 = 64$, which can be expressed as $2^6 = 64$.
Our original equation was $2^{3x} = 64$, so to get 6 as an exponent, we need to multiply 3 by 2.
So, $x = 2$

45) The correct answer is D. Perform the FOIL method on the first two sets of parentheses by multiplying the terms together as shown:
$(x + 1)(x - 2) + (x + 1)^2 - x(x + 1) =$
$(x^2 - 2x + x - 2) + (x + 1)^2 - x(x + 1) =$
$(x^2 - x - 2) + (x + 1)^2 - x(x + 1)$
Then expand $(x + 1)^2$ as shown:
$(x^2 - x - 2) + (x + 1)^2 - x(x + 1) =$
$(x^2 - x - 2) + (x + 1)(x + 1) - x(x + 1) =$
$(x^2 - x - 2) + (x^2 + x + x + 1) - x(x + 1) =$
$x^2 - x - 2 + x^2 + 2x + 1 - (x^2 + x)$

Then group like terms together and factor:
$x^2 - x - 2 + x^2 + 2x + 1 - (x^2 + x) =$
$(x^2 + x^2 - x + 2x - 2 + 1) - x^2 - x =$
$(2x^2 + x - 1) - x^2 - x =$
$2x^2 - x^2 + x - x - 1 =$
$x^2 - 1 =$
$(x + 1)(x - 1)$

46) The correct answer is D.
Step 1: Find the lowest common denominator. We can factor the denominator of the first fraction as follows: $x^2 + x = (x \times x) + (x \times 1) = x(x + 1)$. Since x is common to both denominators, we can convert the denominator of the second fraction to the LCD by multiplying the numerator and denominator of the second fraction by (x + 1).

$$\frac{x^2}{x^2 + x} + \frac{5}{x} =$$

$$\frac{x^2}{x^2 + x} + \left(\frac{5}{x} \times \frac{x + 1}{x + 1}\right) =$$

$$\frac{x^2}{x^2 + x} + \frac{5x + 5}{x^2 + x}$$

Step 2: When you have both fractions in the LCD, add the numerators to solve.

$$\frac{x^2}{x^2 + x} + \frac{5x + 5}{x^2 + x} =$$

$$\frac{x^2 + 5x + 5}{x^2 + x}$$

47) The correct answer is C. Congruent triangles have three equal angles and three equal sides. It is not enough for all three angles of the two triangles to correspond as the sides of the first triangle could be shorter or longer than the sides of the corresponding triangle. To prove that a triangle is congruent, you need to prove that two corresponding sides and two corresponding angles are congruent. We know from the facts of the problem that ∠A is congruent to ∠X. If we also prove that ∠C = ∠Z and side AC = side XZ, then we can conclude that the triangles are congruent. So, answer C is correct.

48) The correct answer is D. The altitude in the original triangle forms a side of each of the two right triangles that are formed. So, each of the right triangles has one side that is 3 feet long. We will call this side B. Half of the base of the triangle forms another side of each of the right triangles. So, each of the right triangles has another side that is 1 foot long because 2 ÷ 2 = 1. We will call this side A.
So, we need to calculate the hypotenuse of these right triangles.
hypotenuse length = $\sqrt{A^2 + B^2}$ =
$\sqrt{1^2 + 3^2}$ = =
$\sqrt{1 + 9}$ = $\sqrt{10}$
The kite is formed of these 4 "hypotenuse" edges, so the perimeter is $4\sqrt{10}$.

49) The correct answer is B. Answer A is incorrect because it has x^2, which will be a parabola when graphed. Answer C is incorrect since the slope will be negative, and the line will decline from left to right. Answer D is incorrect because an equation with an absolute value will result in separate lines in two quadrants of the graph. The graph shows a straight line so, the equation must be in the form y = mx + b. So, B is the correct answer.

50) The correct answer is A. Put the base number inside the radical sign. The denominator of the exponent is the nth root of the radical. The numerator is the new exponent.

$$x^8 = \left(\sqrt[8]{x}\right)^3$$

CHSPE Math Practice Test 7

1) A company measures profits and losses for its four production lines and has recorded the following figures: −14, 52, −36, −7. What was the total profit or loss for all four production lines?
   A) −23
   B) 23
   C) 9
   D) −5

2) A business has already achieved $^9/_{16}$ of its projected sales for this year. Approximately what percentage of the projected sales has already been achieved?
   A) 0.5625%
   B) 5.625%
   C) 56.25%
   D) 43.75%

3) Employee retention rate is calculated by dividing the number of employees who work for a company at the end of the year into the number of employees who worked for the company at the start of the year. Last year, the employee retention rate was 0.95. What percentage best represents the employee retention rate for last year?
   A) 0.95%
   B) 9.50%
   C) 95.0%
   D) 950%

4) Employee loss rate is calculated by dividing the number of employees who left a company during the year into the total number of employees in the company at the start of the year. You had 120 employees at the start of the year, and your employee loss rate was 0.05 for the year. How many employees do you have at the end of the year?
   A) 119
   B) 114
   C) 12
   D) 6

5) A furniture store that sells tables, chairs, and other types of furniture has given a 20 percent discount this month on one of the tables that it sells. This amounts to a discount of $60. What was the original price of the table?
   A) $80
   B) $120
   C) $1200
   D) $300

6) An ice cream store orders ice cream in 10-quart containers. At the start of the day on Wednesday, there were $6^3/_4$ quarts of praline nut ice. At the close of business that Wednesday, there were $2^1/_2$ quarts of praline nut ice cream left. How much praline nut ice cream was sold that day?
A) $4^1/_4$
B) $4^3/_8$
C) $4^5/_8$
D) $4^6/_8$

7) 9 ounces of liquid need to be added to every 6 ounces of active chemical. The current job lot requires 10 ounces of active chemical. How many ounces of liquid should be added?
A) 1.50
B) 15.0
C) 0.67
D) 67.0

8) Susan wanted to find the mean of the six surveys she administered this month. However, she erroneously divided the total points from the six surveys by 5, which gave her a result of 96. What is the correct mean of her six surveys?
A) 63
B) 80
C) 82
D) 91

9) A bakery makes brownies, cakes, and other confections every day. It allows employees to take home the goods that have not sold by the close of business each day. There are 3 partial trays of unsold brownies at the end of the day, and each tray has $^1/_8$ of the brownies left in it. These brownies need to be divided among four employees. What amount below represents the fraction of a tray of brownies that each employee will receive?
A) $^1/_6$
B) $^{32}/_3$
C) $^3/_{32}$
D) $^3/_{24}$

10) Consider three particular items. Item A weighs $14^3/_4$ pounds, Item B weighs $20^1/_5$ pounds, and Item C weighs 36.35 pounds. What is the total weight for these three items?
A) 71.30
B) 71.05
C) 71.15
D) 71.25

11) An office purchased 50 reams of paper this month. At the end of the month, 5 of these reams of paper have been used. Which decimal figure below best expresses the amount of reams of paper that have been used in relation to the amount of reams that were purchased?
A) 0.0010
B) 0.0100
C) 0.1000
D) 0.0500

12) One hundred prospective candidates took an aptitude test for a new job opening. The 55 female candidates had an average score of 87, while the 45 male candidates had an average of 80. What was the average aptitude test score for all 100 candidates?
A) 82.00
B) 83.15
C) 83.50
D) 83.85

13) Chain-link fence is sold by the 1/2 yard. Each 1/2 yard sells for $10.50. One customer buys $20^1/_2$ yards of this particular type of fence. How much will the customer pay for this purchase?
A) $215.25
B) $225.75
C) $430.50
D) $450.50

14) $49^3/_{16}$ inches of rope is needed to finish one job and $18^1/_{16}$ inches is needed for another. How many inches of rope are needed in order to complete both jobs?
A) $66^1/_8$
B) $67^1/_8$
C) $66^1/_4$
D) $67^1/_4$

15) 11 out of 132 SIM cards are defective. What percentage best represents the amount of defective SIM cards in relation to the total?
A) 0.08%
B) 8%
C) 83%
D) 92%

16) To make soda-bread biscuits, the best proportion of baking soda to flour is 2 to 9. A batch of soda-bread biscuits calls for 126 cups of flour. How many cups of baking soda should be used?
A) 28
B) 18
C) 14
D) 7

17) Marsha worked from 12:10 PM to 2:25 PM knitting 3 caps by hand from alpaca yarn. At this rate, how many caps will she knit during a 9-hour period?
A) 6
B) 12
C) 36
D) 27

18) Market research shows that 58% of your customers are 10 to 20 pounds overweight and 27% of your customers are 21 to 30 pounds overweight. What percentage below represents the number of customers that are 10 to 30 pounds overweight?
A) 27%
B) 31%

C) 75%
D) 85%

19) If a circle has a radius of 4, what equation can be used to calculate the approximate circumference of the circle?
A) 3.14 ÷ 8
B) 3.14 ÷ 16
C) 8 × 3.14
D) 16 × 3.14

20) If a circle has a radius of 6, what equation can be used to calculate the area of the circle?
A) 6 × 3.14
B) 12 × 3.14
C) 24 × 3.14
D) 36 × 3.14

21) If circle A has a radius of 0.4 and circle B has a radius of 0.2, what is the difference in area between the two circles?
A) 0.1256
B) 0.3768
C) 0.5024
D) 1.256

22) A rectangular box has a base that is 5 inches wide and 6 inches long. The height of the box is 10 inches. What is the volume of the box in cubic inches?
A) 30
B) 110
C) 150
D) 300

23) Find the area of the right triangle whose base is 2 and height is 5.
A) 2.5
B) 5
C) 10
D) 15

24) Find the approximate volume of a cone which has a radius of 3 and a height of 4.
A) 12.56
B) 37.68
C) 4.1762
D) 2.355

25) A circular pond has a diameter of 36 feet. What figure below best approximates the area of the pond?
A) 1017
B) 804
C) 113
D) 57

26) You need to report the amount of the average high temperature in your town over a three-month period in degrees Fahrenheit. However, the high temperatures are reported in Celsius. You have received the following data: January: 12°C; February: 13°C; March 17°C. What was the average high temperature for these three months in degrees Fahrenheit?
A) 57.2
B) 62.6
C) 82.8
D) 25.8

27) A recent report states that 72.8% of the construction for a shopping center is now completed, and it has taken 182 days to do so. If work continues at the same rate, approximately how many more days will be needed to finish the construction?
A) 17
B) 18
C) 58
D) 68

28) A dance judge awards a number from 1 to 10 to score dancers during a TV show. During one show, he judged five dancers and awarded the following scores: 9.9, 9.9, 8.2, 7.6 and 6.8. What was the median value of his scores for this show?
A) 8.2
B) 8.48
C) 9.9
D) 3.1

29) A doctor measures the pulse for several patients one morning. She recorded these results: 54, 68, 62, 60, 75, 58, 84, and 91. What is the range for this group of patients?
A) 30
B) 37
C) 65
D) 69

30) What is the value of $f_1(2)$ where $f_1(x) = 49^{1/x}$?
A) $\sqrt{7}$
B) $49/2$
C) $49/\sqrt{x}$
D) 7

31) What is the range of $y = -5x^4 + 8$?
A) $y \geq -8$
B) $y \leq -8$
C) $y \leq 8$
D) $y \geq 8$

32) Perform the operation and simplify: $\dfrac{3a^2}{4} \times \dfrac{2}{a^3} = ?$

A) $\dfrac{3}{2a}$

B) $\dfrac{5a^2}{4a^3}$

C) $\dfrac{8}{3a^5}$

D) $\dfrac{8}{3a^6}$

33) Which of the following is an equation of a line that is perpendicular to the one above shown below?

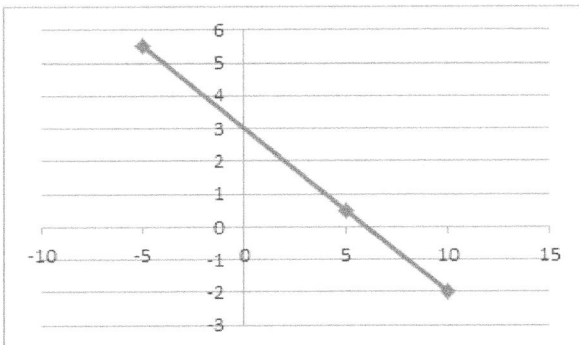

A) $y = \frac{1}{2}x + 3$
B) $y = 2x + 3$
C) $y = -x + 3$
D) $y = -\frac{1}{2}x + 3$

34) Express in scientific notation: 12,567
   A) 1.2567×10^4
   B) 1.2567×10^{-4}
   C) $1.2567 = \log_4 10$
   D) $1.2567 = \log_{10} 4$

35) Solve for x: $x^2 - 11x < -24$
   A) $3 < x > 8$
   B) $3 < x < 8$
   C) $3 > x > 8$
   D) $3 > x < 8$

36) Which of the following is a function where y = f(x)?

A)

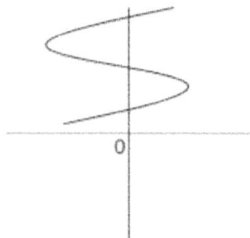

B)

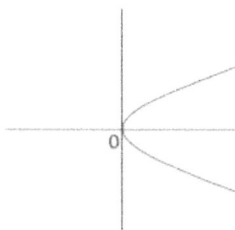

C)

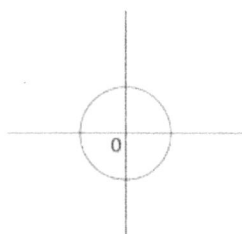

D)

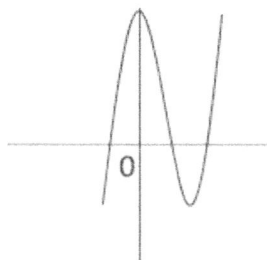

37) If $3 + 4(2\sqrt{x} + 5) = 55$, then $\sqrt{x}$ = ?
A) 2
B) 16
C) 4
D) $^2/_3$

38) Find an equivalent for the following: $\sqrt{7}$

A) $7^{\frac{1}{4}}$

B) $1^{\sqrt{7}}$

C) $7^{\frac{1}{2}}$

D) 7^0

39) The graph of y = f(x) is show below.

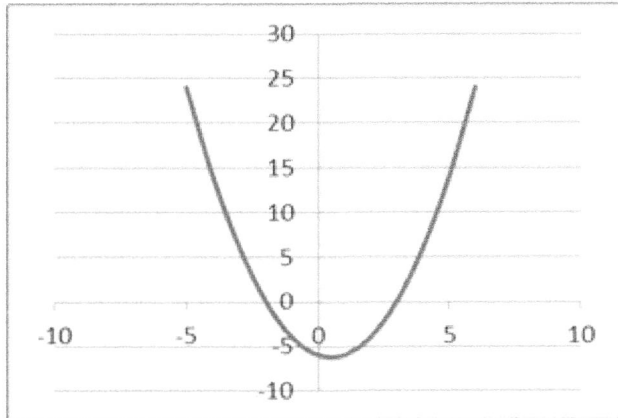

Which of the following equations could define f(x)?
A) f(x) = (x − 3)(x + 2)
B) f(x) = (x + 3)(x + 2)
C) f(x) = (−2x − 3)(x + 2)
D) f(x) = (−x − 3)(x + 2)

40) Circle A has a radius of 6. Circle B has a radius of 14. What is the difference between the area of circle B and the area of circle A?
A) 64π
B) 160π
C) 36π
D) 196π

41) Express in scientific notation: 0.006872
A) 6.872×10^3
B) 6.872×10^{-3}
C) $6.872 = \log_3 10$
D) $6.872 = \log_{10} 3$

42) $(15a^2 + 22a + 8) \div (3a + 2) = ?$
A) 5a + 5
B) 5a + 8
C) 5a + 4
D) 5a + 2

43) Examine the illustration below and answer the question that follows.

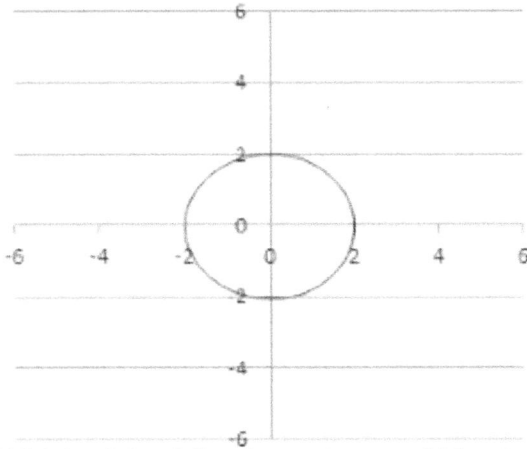

Which of the following points could be the intersection of the circle and the line x = –2?
A) (0,–2)
B) (2, 0)
C) (0, 2)
D) (–2, 0)

44) Factor the following equation: $x^2 + 3x – 10 = 0$
A) $(x + 5)(x – 2) = 0$
B) $(x + 2)(x – 5) = 0$
C) $(x + 3)(x – 10) = 0$
D) $x(x + 3 – 10) = 0$

45) Solve for x and y: 6x + 3y = 24 and 10x + 6y = 24
A) x = 2 and y = 2
B) x = –12 and y = 16
C) x = 2 and y = 4
D) x = 12 and y = –16

46) Consider the quadratic function $(x) = ax^2 + bx – c$, where $f(x) = y$. If m equals zero, how many real number solutions exist for the following equation: $ax^2 + bx – c = mx$?
A) 0
B) 1
C) 2
D) Cannot be determined.

47) If 5P + 3Q = R, then P = ?
A) $P = {}^{R-3Q}/_5$
B) $P = {}^{R-5}/_{3Q}$
C) $P = {}^5/_{R-3Q}$
D) $P = {}^{3Q}/_{R-5}$

48) If the radius of a circle is 3 and the radians of the subtended angle measure $\pi/3$, what is the length of the arc subtending the central angle?
A) $\pi/3$
B) $\pi/9$
C) π
D) 3π

49) In triangle XYZ, ∠X is a right angle. Side XY is 9 units long, side XZ is 12 units long. How long is side YZ.
A) 9
B) 15
C) 17
D) Cannot be determined.

50) The rectangular cuboid in the illustration below has a length of 16 centimeters (cm), a width of 14 cm, and a volume of 2,016 cubic cm. If the length width and height are each increased by 20%, what is the volume of the enlarged cuboid in cubic centimeters?

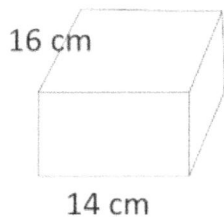

16 cm

14 cm

A) 2903.04
B) 2419.20
C) 3483.648
D) 2036.00

Answers and Explanations for CHSPE Math Practice Test 7

1) The correct answer is D. Add the gains and subtract the setbacks as shown:
$-14 + 52 - 36 - 7 = -5$

2) The correct answer is C. Divide and then express the result as a percentage. Step 1 – Treat the line in the fraction as the division symbol: $9/16 = 9 \div 16 = 0.5625$. Step 2 – To express the result from Step 1 as a percentage, move the decimal point two places to the right and add the percent sign: $0.5625 = 56.25\%$

3) The correct answer is C. Move the decimal point two places to the right and add the percent sign: $0.95 = 95.0\%$

4) The correct answer is B. Subtract the decimal from 1 to find the decimal amount left: $1 - 0.05 = 0.95$. Then multiply the total number of employees at the start of the year by this decimal number: $120 \times 0.95 = 114$ employees left

5) The correct answer is D. 20 percent is equal to 0.20. We are doing a reverse percentage, so we need to divide to solve: $\$60 \div 0.20 = \$300$. We can check this result as follows: $300 \times 0.20 = 60$

6) The correct answer is A. First, subtract whole numbers: $6 - 2 = 4$. Then subtract fractions: $^3/_4 - ^1/_2 = ^3/_4 - ^2/_4 = ^1/_4$. Put them together for the result: $4^1/_4$

7) The correct answer is B. Set up the proportion as a fraction: 9 ounces of liquid for every 6 of ounces active chemical $= ^9/_6$. Then simplify the fraction: $^9/_6 \div ^3/_3 = ^3/_2$. Now, multiply the fraction by the amount for the current job to solve: $^3/_2 \times 10 = ^{30}/_2 = 30 \div 2 = 15$

8) The correct answer is B. First you need to find the total points. You do this by taking the erroneous average times 5: $5 \times 96 = 480$. Then you need to divide the total points earned by the correct number of surveys to get the correct average: $480 \div 6 = 80$

9) The correct answer is C. You have 3 partial trays of unsold brownies at the end of the day, and each tray has $^1/_8$ of the brownies left in it, so in total you have $^3/_8$ of a tray left. You need to divide this by 4 employees. When you are asked to divide fractions, remember that you need to invert the second fraction. Here we have the whole number 4. 4 inverted is $^1/_4$. So, multiply the fractions to solve: $^3/_8 \times ^1/_4 = ^{(3 \times 1)}/_{(8 \times 4)} = ^3/_{32}$

10) The correct answer is A. Represent the mixed numbers as decimal numbers. Item 1: $14^3/_4 = 14.75$; Item 2: $20^1/_5 = 20.20$; Item 3: 36.35. Then add all three amounts together to find the total: $14.75 + 20.20 + 36.35 = 71.30$

11) The correct answer is C. The office purchased 50 reams of paper this month and has used 5 of them, so you need to divide to solve $5 \div 50 = 0.10$

12) The correct answer is D. First of all, you have to calculate the total amount of points earned by the entire group. Multiply the female average by the number of female candidates. Total points for females: $87 \times 55 = 4785$. Then multiply the male average by the number of males. Total points for male candidates: $80 \times 45 = 3600$. Then add these two amounts together to find out the total points scored by the entire group. Total points for entire group: $4785 + 3600 = 8385$. When you have calculated the total amount of points for the entire

group, you divide this by the total number of candidates to get the average: 8385 ÷ 100 = 83.85

13) The correct answer is C. Step 1 – Determine the price per yard: $10.50 per 1/2 yard × 2 = $21.00 per yard. Step 2 – Calculate the price for 20 yards: 20 × $21.00 = $420.00. Step 3 – The customer purchased 20 and a half yards, so the price of the remaining half yard is $10.50. Add this to the result from Step 2 to get your answer: $420.00 + $10.50 = $430.50

14) The correct answer is D. Step 1 – Add the whole numbers: 49 + 18 = 67. Step 2 – Add the fractions: 3/16 + 1/16 = 4/16 = 1/4. Step 3 – Combine the results from Step 1 and Step 2 to get your new mixed number to solve the problem: 67 + 1/4 = $67^1/_4$

15) The correct answer is B. Take the amount of defective SIM cards and divide by the total amount of SIM cards: 11 ÷ 132 = 0.083 = 8.3%, which we round to 8%.

16) The correct answer is A. Step 1 – Take the total amount of flour required for this batch and divide by the 9 stated in the original ratio: 126 ÷ 9 = 14. Step 2 – Take the amount from Step 1 and multiply by 2 from the original ratio to solve the problem: 14 × 2 = 28

17) The correct answer is B. Step 1 – Calculate the amount of time spent on the initial job: 12:10 to 2:25 = 2 hours and 15 minutes = 135 minutes. Step 2 – Calculate the rate per cap: 135 minutes ÷ 3 caps = 45 minutes per cap. Step 3 – Calculate how many minutes there are in 9 hours: 9 hours × 60 minutes = 540 minutes. Step 4 – Divide to solve: 540 minutes available ÷ 45 minutes per cap = 12 caps

18) The correct answer is D. Add the percentages together to solve: 58% + 27% = 85%

19) The correct answer is C. The circumference of a circle is calculated by using this formula: Circumference ≈ 3.14 × diameter. The diameter of a circle is always equal to the radius times 2. So, the diameter for this circle is 4 × 2 = 8. Therefore, the approximate circumference is: 3.14 × 8 = 25.12

20) The correct answer is D. Area of a circle ≈ 3.14 × radius^2. The radius of this circle is 6, and 6^2 = 36. Therefore, the area is approximately: 36 × 3.14 = 113.04

21) The correct answer is B. The area of circle A is 0.4^2 × 3.14 = 0.16 × 3.14 = 0.5024. The area of circle B is 0.2^2 × 3.14 = 0.04 × 3.14 = 0.1256. Then subtract: 0.5024 – 0.1256 = 0.3768

22) The correct answer is D. The volume of a box is calculated by taking the length times the width times the height: 5 × 6 × 10 = 300

23) The correct answer is B. Triangle area = (base × height) ÷ 2. Substitute the amounts for base and height: area = (5 × 2) ÷ 2 = 10 ÷ 2 = 5

24) The correct answer is B. Cone volume = (3.14 × radius^2 × height) ÷ 3. Substitute the values for base and height.
volume = (3.14 × 3^2 × 4) ÷ 3 = (3.14 × 9 × 4) ÷ 3 = 3.14 × 36 ÷ 3 = 37.68
Now calculate the square footage of the new rooms:
20 × 10 = 200

2 rooms × (10 × 8) = 160
200 + 160 = 360 total square feet for the new rooms

So, the remaining square footage for the bathroom is calculated by taking the total minus the square footage of the new rooms: 400 − 360 = 40 square feet left. Since each existing room is 10 feet long, we know that the new bathroom also needs to be 10 feet long in order to fit in. So, the new bathroom measures 4 feet × 10 feet.

25) The correct answer is A. The area of a circle is 3.14 × radius². Radius is half of diameter, and in our problem the diameter is 36, so the radius is 18. So, put the values into the formula to solve: 3.14 × 18 × 18 = 1,017

26) The correct answer is A. Step 1 – Calculate the average high temperature in Celsius: (12 + 13 + 17) ÷ 3 = 42 ÷ 3 = 14°C average. Step 2 – Convert the average in Celsius to Fahrenheit using the formula provided. °F = 1.8(°C) + 32 = 1.8(14°) + 32 = 25.2 + 32 = 57.2° F.

27) The correct answer is D. Step 1 – Calculate the rate in terms of a daily percentage: 72.8% ÷ 182 days = 0.4% per day. Step 2 – Divide this amount into 100% to find the approximate number of days in total: 100% ÷ 0.4% per day = 250 days in total. Step 3 – Subtract to determine how many days remain: 250 − 182 = 68 days left

28) The correct answer is A. The scores were: 9.9, 9.9, 8.2, 7.6 and 6.8. Put them in ascending order and highlight the one in the middle: 6.8, 7.6, **8.2**, 9.9, 9.9

29) The correct answer is B. The range is the highest amount minus the lowest amount: 91 − 54 = 37

30) The correct answer is D. In our function x = 2, so put in the value of 2 for x in the function: $49^{1/x} = 49^{1/2}$. A number to the power of one-half is the same as the square root of the number: $49^{1/x} = \sqrt{49} = \sqrt{7 \times 7} = 7$

31) The correct answer is C. Remember that the range is the output, or the value of y, for a function. Any positive or negative number to the power of four will result in a positive number. When x^4 is multiplied by −5, the product will always be negative, except when x is equal to zero. When x = 0, the result is 8. So, the range is: y ≤ 8

32) The correct answer is A. Multiply the numerator of the first fraction by the numerator of the second fraction to get the new numerator. Then multiply the denominators:
$$\frac{3a^2}{4} \times \frac{2}{a^3} =$$
$$\frac{3a^2 \times 2}{4 \times a^3} =$$
$$\frac{6a^2}{4a^3}$$
Then find the greatest common factor and cancel out to simplify:
$$\frac{6a^2}{4a^3}$$

$$\frac{2 \times 3 \times a \times a}{2 \times 2 \times a \times a \times a} =$$

$$\frac{\cancel{2} \times 3 \times \cancel{a} \times \cancel{a}}{\cancel{2} \times 2 \times \cancel{a} \times \cancel{a} \times a} = \frac{3}{2a}$$

33) The correct answer is A. For questions on graphs like this one, look first of all to see which coordinates are the most clearly identifiable. We can see the point (0, 3) clearly, which is the y-intercept. We can also see point (10, −2). Our coordinates are: (0, 3) and (10, −2) The formula for slope is: $^{rise}/_{run} = ^{y_2 - y_1}/_{x_2 - x_1}$. Substitute the values for the coordinates: $^{-2-3}/_{10-0} = ^{-5}/_{10} = -^{1}/_{2}$. The slopes of perpendicular lines are negative reciprocals of each other. So, to get the negative reciprocal the line, you invert the fraction to make an integer and then change the sign from negative to positive. The slope for the perpendicular line is the negative reciprocal of $-^{1}/_{2}$, which is 2. So, an equation for a perpendicular line is: y = 2x + 3

34) The correct answer is B. In this problem, we have a decimal number greater than 1, and for scientific notation, we need to make the first number between 1 and 10, so we need to use 1.2567 as our first number. We have to move the decimal to the left, so we need to use a positive exponent. The decimal is moved four places, so our exponent is 4. So, our result is: 1.2567×10^4

35) The correct answer is B. Isolate the integers to the left side of the inequality to get 0 on the right:
$x^2 - 11x < -24$
$x^2 - 11x + 24 < -24 + 24$
$x^2 - 11x + 24 < 0$
When you have the quadratic in this form, you can factor it. The factors of 24 are: 1 × 24, 2 × 12, 3 × 8, and 4 × 6. We need to find the two factors that add up to − 11, so we need −3 and −8. Then express the inequality as a factored quadratic: (x − 3)(x − 8) < 0
Then find the values of x that satisfy the quadratic. You do this by putting in zero for the x in each set of parentheses.
(x − 3)(x − 8) < 0
(0 − 3)(x − 8) < 0
x < 8

(x − 3)(x − 8) < 0
(x − 3)(0 − 8) < 0
3 < x

Then express in an inequality to solve:
3 < x < 8

36) The correct answer is D. Functions have one output value for each input value.
So, each value of x, a function will yield only one corresponding value of y. Graphs A, B, and C have more than one corresponding value of y for certain values of x, so they are not functions.

37) The correct answer is C.
Deal with the integer first:
$3 + 4(2\sqrt{x} + 5) = 55$

$3 - 3 + 4(2\sqrt{x} + 5) = 55 - 3$

$4(2\sqrt{x} + 5) = 52$

Then perform multiplication on the terms in parentheses:

$4(2\sqrt{x} + 5) = 52$

$8\sqrt{x} + 20 = 52$

$8\sqrt{x} + 20 - 20 = 52 - 20$

$8\sqrt{x} = 32$

Then divide to get rid of the integer in front of the radical sign:

$8\sqrt{x} = 32$

$8\sqrt{x} \div 8 = 32 \div 8$

$\sqrt{x} = 4$

38) The correct answer is C. Remember the following principle: $\sqrt{x} = x^{\frac{1}{2}}$

So, the answer is: $\sqrt{7} = 7^{\frac{1}{2}}$

39) The correct answer is A. The graph opens upward, so the equation defining $f(x)$ must have a positive leading coefficient. The graph includes coordinates (–5, 24), (0, –6), and (6, 24), all of which satisfy equation A. The coordinates do not satisfy equation B, and equations C and D have negative leading coefficients, so A is the correct answer.

40) The correct answer is B. Do not be tempted to subtract the radii and then put this difference into the circle area formula. You need to calculate the area of each circle and then subtract these two results.
Area of circle A = $\pi R^2 = \pi 6^2 = 36\pi$
Area of circle B = $\pi R^2 = \pi 14^2 = 196\pi$
Then subtract: $196\pi - 36\pi = 160\pi$

41) The correct answer is B. In this problem, we have a decimal number less than 1, and for scientific notation, we need to make the first number between 1 and 10, so we need to use 6.872 as our first number. We have to move the decimal to the right, so we need to use a negative exponent. The decimal is moved three places, so our exponent is –3. So, our result is: 6.872×10^{-3}

42) The correct answer is C. Perform long division on the polynomial as shown below:

$$\begin{array}{r} 5a + 4 \\ 3a + 2\overline{)15a^2 + 22a + 8} \\ \underline{-(15a^2 + 10a)} \\ 12a + 8 \\ \underline{-(12a + 8)} \\ 0 \end{array}$$

43) The correct answer is D. The line x = –2 is vertical and parallel to the y-axis. So, the point of intersection with the circle also needs to have a x coordinate of –2. Coordinates (–2, 0) meet these criteria.

44) The correct answer is A. Our original equation was: $x^2 + 3x - 10 = 0$
Step 1: Look at the third term of the equation, which is –10. Find two integers that equal –10 when multiplied.

$1 \times -10 = -10$
$2 \times -5 = -10$
$5 \times -2 = -10$
$10 \times -1 = -10$
Step 2: Look at the second term of the equation, which is 3x. Find two integers from Step 1 that equal 3 when they are added.
$5 + -2 = 3$
Step 3: Use the integers 5 and –2 to factor our quadratic.
$(x + 5)(x - 2) = 0$

45) The correct answer is D. Our equations were $6x + 3y = 24$ and $10x + 6y = 24$. We need to get the same coefficient on one of the terms in order to eliminate the term. So, multiply the first equation by 2 to get 6y in the first equation:
$6x + 3y = 24$
$(6x \times 2) + (3y \times 2) = (24 \times 2)$
$12x + 6y = 48$
Now perform the elimination method by subtracting the second equation from this result.
$$
\begin{array}{r}
12x + 6y = 48 \\
-(10x + 6y = 24) \\
\hline
2x \qquad = 24 \\
x \qquad = 12
\end{array}
$$
Now substitute the value of x to solve for y.
$x = 12$
$6x + 3y = 24$
$(6 \times 12) + 3y = 24$
$72 + 3y = 24$
$72 - 72 + 3y = 24 - 72$
$3y = 24 - 72$
$3y = -48$
$3y \div 3 = -48 \div 3$
$y = -16$

46) The correct answer is C. The quadratic can be factored in the format: $(ax - b)(x + c) = 0$. To solve, we need to get either of the parentheticals to be equal to zero. Therefore, two real number solutions exist for the above equation.

47) The correct answer is A. Perform inverse operations to isolate P:
$5P + 3Q = R$
$5P + 3Q - 3Q = R - 3Q$
$5P = R - 3Q$
$5 \times P = R - 3Q$
$5 \div 5 \times P = (R - 3Q) \div 5$
$P = (R - 3Q) \div 5$
$P = {}^{R - 3Q}/_5$

48) The correct answer is C. One radian is the measurement of an angle at the center of a circle which is subtended by an arc that is equal in length to the radius of the circle. These symbols are used in questions on radians:
θ = the radians of the subtended angle
s = arc length

119

COPYRIGHT 2023. Test Prep Guides dba www.test-prep-guides.com
This material may not be copied or reproduced in any form.

r = radius

The following formulas can be used for calculations with radians:

$\theta = s \div r$

$s = r\theta$

Use the second formula from above, and substitute values to solve the problem.

In our problem:

radius (r) = 3

radians (θ) = $\pi/3$

$s = r\theta$

$s = 3 \times \pi/3$

$s = \pi$

49) The correct answer is B. We need to calculate the hypotenuse of the right triangle.

hypotenuse length = $\sqrt{A^2 + B^2}$ =

$\sqrt{9^2 + 12^2} = =$

$\sqrt{81 + 144} = \sqrt{225} = 15$

50) The correct answer is C.

The volume of a cuboid is:

length × width × height

The length is 12 cm and the width is 14 cm, so put in the values and work the formula in reverse to find the height:

2,016 = 16 × 14 × height

2,016 ÷ 16 ÷ 14 = height

9 = height

The length width and height are each increased by 20%, so find the new measurements:

length = 16 × 1.20 = 19.2

width = 14 × 1.20 = 16.8

height = 9 × 1.20 = 10.8

Then multiply these three amounts together to get the volume of the enlarged cuboid:

19.2 × 16.8 × 10.8 = 3483.648

Made in the USA
Las Vegas, NV
10 February 2025